PRENTICE-HALL FOUNDATIONS OF MODERN LINGUISTICS SERIES

Sanford A. Schane
editor

Introduction to Contemporary Linguistic Semantics

GEORGE L. DILLON

*Indiana University-Purdue University
at Fort Wayne*

PRENTICE-HALL, INC., ENGLEWOOD CLIFFS, NEW JERSEY 07632

Library of Congress Cataloging in Publication Data

DILLON, GEORGE L   date
    Introduction to contemporary linguistic semantics.

    (Prentice-Hall foundations of modern linguistics
series)
    Bibliography: p.
    1. Semantics. I. Title.
P325.D54   412   76-41853
ISBN 0-13-479451-6

© 1977 PRENTICE-HALL, INC., Englewood Cliffs, New Jersey 07632

Printed in the United States of America

10 9 8 7 6 5 4 3 2 1

PRENTICE-HALL INTERNATIONAL, INC., LONDON
PRENTICE-HALL OF AUSTRALIA PTY. LTD., SYDNEY
PRENTICE-HALL OF CANADA, LTD., TORONTO
PRENTICE-HALL OF INDIA PRIVATE LIMITED, NEW DELHI
PRENTICE-HALL OF JAPAN, INC., TOKYO
PRENTICE-HALL OF SOUTHEAST ASIA PTE. LTD., SINGAPORE
WHITEHALL BOOKS LIMITED, WELLINGTON, NEW ZEALAND

*For Sharon, who still thinks pots
are the same as pans*

Editor's Note

Language permeates human interaction, culture, behavior, and thought. The *Foundations of Modern Linguistics Series* focuses on current research in the nature of language.

Linguistics as a discipline has undergone radical change within the last decade. Questions raised by today's linguists are not necessarily those asked previously by traditional grammarians or by structural linguists. Most of the available introductory texts on linguistics, having been published several years ago, cannot be expected to portray the colorful contemporary scene. Nor is there a recent book surveying the spectrum of modern linguistic research, probably because the field is still moving too fast, and no one author can hope to capture the diverse moods reflected in the various areas of linguistic inquiry. But it does not seem unreasonable now to ask individual specialists to provide a picture of how they view their own particular field of interest. With the *Foundations of Modern Linguistics Series* we will attempt to organize the kaleidoscopic present-day scene. Teachers in search of up-to-date materials can choose individual volumes of the series for courses in linguistics and in the nature of language.

If linguistics is no longer what it was ten years ago its relation to other disciplines has also changed. Language is peculiarly human and it is found deep inside the mind. Consequently, the problems of modern linguistics are equally of concern to anthropology, sociology, psychology, and philosophy. Linguistics has always had a close affiliation with literature and with foreign language learning. Developments in other areas have had their impact on linguistics. There are mathematical models of language and formalisms of its structure. Computers are being used to test grammars. Other sophisticated instrumentation has revolutionized research in phonetics. Advances in neurology have contributed to our understanding of language pathologies and to the development of language. This series is also intended, then, to acquaint other disciplines with the progress going on in linguistics.

Finally, we return to our first statement. Language permeates our lives. We sincerely hope that the *Foundations of Modern Linguistics Series* will be of interest to anyone wanting to know what language is and how it affects us.

Sanford A. Schane, *editor*

Contents

VI

Negatives, Quantifiers, and Connectives in Logic and Language

83

VII

Pragmatics

99

Preface

The title of this book attempts to make three specifications: first, the book is about what linguists call semantics; second, it is concerned almost entirely with work done in the last fifteen years; third, it assumes no background in logic or syntax. Its first objective is to develop accuracy, subtlety, and finesse in describing senses of words and readings of sentences. In this regard, a better title might have contained the word *preliminaries*. Generative grammar assumes that readings are related to sentences in regular ways, and it tries to make the rules relating them explicit; here I have only indicated informally what some of those rules must do. Noam Chomsky suggested a few years ago that a reasonable choice between competing formalisms must wait on progress in descriptive semantics, and I hope that this book may in a very modest way contribute to that progress.

One of the most exciting aspects of semantics presently is that it is the focus of work in the disciplines of logic, philosophy, psychology, and artificial intelligence as well as linguistics. The work being done by psycholinguists is particularly important if we want to claim that semantics represents the actual (as opposed to merely potential) knowledge that speakers have acquired. I have described the psychological studies of basic points as much as limitations of space and my learning will permit (both are severe). For a similar reason, I have described dictionaries in some detail because they constitute vast, irreplaceable funds of information about how people have actually used words.

I have drawn most heavily on the works of John M. Anderson, Dwight Bolinger, Wallace L. Chafe, Charles J. Fillmore, George Lakoff, and James D. McCawley. Any misconstruction of their writings is, of course, my own responsibility. Various persons have read portions of the manuscript and offered helpful comments: the most numerous group are my students in G205 at Indiana University-Purdue University at Ft. Wayne. David L. Fairchild and Frederick Kirchhoff read Chapters VI and II, respectively, and the anonymous readers for Prentice-Hall made many useful observations. Finally, my wife Sharon and daughter Jennifer have been deeply involved in this work—both have shown me things that I otherwise would never have seen.

George L. Dillon

Acknowledgments

Citations from *The American Heritage Dictionary of the English Language* © 1969, 1970, 1971, 1973, 1975, 1976, Houghton Mifflin Company. Reprinted by permission of Houghton Mifflin Company.

Citations from *Webster's New Collegiate Dictionary* © 1976 by G. & C. Merriam Co., Publishers of the Merriam-Webster Dictionaries. Reprinted by permission of G. & C. Merriam Company.

Citations from *The Shorter Oxford English Dictionary*, 3rd ed. 1944, edited by C. T. Onions. By permission of Oxford University Press.

Citations from *The Complete Pelican Shakespeare*, General Editor: Alfred Harbage; *Othello* edited by Gerald Eades Bentley; *Antony and Cleopatra* edited by Maynard Mack (New York: Penguin Books, 1969). Copyright © Penguin Books Inc. 1969. Reprinted by permission of Penguin Books.

Citations from *The Random House College Dictionary*, revised edition (1975), by permission of Random House, Inc.

Citations from "Two Songs from a Play" from *The Collected Poems* of W. B. Yeats, reprinted by permission of M. B. Yeats and Miss Anne Yeats and The Macmillan Company of London and Basingstoke. Reprinted with permission of Macmillan Publishing Co., Inc. Copyright 1928 by Macmillan Publishing Co., Inc., renewed 1956 by Georgia Yeats.

Introduction to Contemporary Linguistic Semantics

The Meaning of a Word

The Domain of Semantics

Most writers on semantics would agree that it is the study of meanings. This is probably the only statement about the subject that all would subscribe to, and disagreement begins with what is properly meant by *meaning*. Nonetheless, a number of linguists have in recent years come to a shared understanding of what they would like to explain, and this program will provide the central focus of this book. Essentially, they propose to explicate the knowledge speakers must have to be able to make the following judgments about words and sentences of the language:

(a) that many words are **ambiguous** over more than one **sense** and hence that some sentences containing them can be taken more than one way:

> He dusted the plants. ('put it on' or 'took it off')
> She watered them. ('diluted' or 'nourished')
> He is a tiger. (two- or four-legged)

(b) that various words in certain combinations are incongruous or **anomalous:**

> They amused the tulips.
> Green ideas sleep furiously.

(c) that certain combinations are **contradictory:**

> colorless red fabric
> accidentally chase

(d) that certain combinations are **redundant:**

> intentionally murder
> male uncle
> scrutinize carefully
> circumnavigate around

(e) that certain words share one or more elements of meaning—they are
   related in meaning:

> chase, follow, pursue
> embezzle, pilfer, filch, shoplift

(f) that a special case of relatedness exists where some words are more
   specific than more general words:

> parent—father
> cut—snip
> take—steal—embezzle

(g) that sentences have logical relations to other sentences—some **entail**
   other sentences:

> She killed him. He died.

> some sentences are **equivalent** in truth-value:

> The book is underneath the pillow. The pillow is on top of the book.

(h) that an element of meaning, while not strictly part of the meaning of a
   word, is usually **associated** with it, or sometimes associated with it:

> Tigers are (usually) fierce.

One assumes that making these judgments draws on knowledge of the
meanings of the words involved (plus knowledge about how these meanings
are combined in sentences), and insofar as speakers agree in their judgments
of particular cases (and they don't always) this knowledge is the same in the
mind of each speaker.
   Two facts about this knowledge are evident at the outset. First, word

meanings cannot be unanalyzable wholes, each one arbitrarily different from every other, or judgments of relatedness and entailment could not be made. Second, judgments of anomaly and contradiction can be made with regard to whole classes of items: *colorless blue fabric* is as bad as *colorless red fabric, accidentally commit perjury* is as bad as *accidentally chase.* A major portion of modern linguistic semantics is devoted to finding the most general and explicit terms for analyzing this knowledge. A lot of it is represented in a scattered and implicit way in dictionaries—semantics aims at making it explicit and showing the general patterns. The most general and explicit analysis is not guaranteed to be psychologically the most real, however, for at least two reasons: one is that people undoubtedly differ in the degree to which they maximize the generality and simplicity of their codings of word meanings ("verbal aptitude" tests measure this); the other is that there may be alternative analyses that maximize generality in other areas of vocabulary, though not in the area in which we are looking. One person told me that she had always analyzed *telegraph* as 'communicate a written message (electro)mechanically' (linking it with *write* and *telephone*) rather than 'write at a distance' (linking it with *telephone, telescope, teletype*). Whether one analyzes *telegraph* her way or the other way does not affect the truth-value of *telegraph.* Both analyses, for example, can account for the contradiction in

I kept your location secret though I telegraphed it to the FBI.

Obviously one cannot make substantive claims about maximum generality and simplicity until whole vocabularies have been analyzed, and the accomplishment of this task lies very far in the future. The classic studies in descriptive semantics have been done in what appear to be fairly clearly bounded "fields" such as kinship terms, adjectival and prepositional meanings, causative and inchoative verbs, verbs of judging and verbs of cooking, and even with these there arise problems of psychological reality. Still, there is no question that the impulse to analyze and generalize is one very strong component in the human cognitive apparatus—the virtually exclusive concentration on its operation in the following pages may be one-sided, but surely not totally wrong-headed.

1.2

Sameness and Difference
of Meaning

When people speak of the meaning of a word, they are usually speaking about one of its senses (corresponding roughly to the numbered subdivisions of a dictionary entry), usually what they believe is the primary or central sense. They do not mean to generalize on what all the senses have in common. It is not always obvious, however, how many different senses should be discriminated for a word, or whether a word in two sentences is being used in the same or different senses (or whether, indeed, it is the same word —see Glossary: **word**). Linguists have developed "gapping" and "pronominalization" tests based on the fact that words can be gapped and pronominalized in conjoined sentences only when they are used in the same sense. When they are used in different senses, the effect is that of a pun. For example,

> John watered the plants, and Mary watered the lawn.

can be gapped to

> John watered the plants, and Mary, the lawn.

but the effect of

> John watered the plants, and Mary, the drinks.

is mildly humorous, giving rise to the conclusion that *water* in *water the drinks* is used in a different sense ('dilute by adding water to') from that of the first *water* ('nourish by applying water to'). On the other hand, using *paint* to mean 'protect by applying paint to' and to mean 'decorate by applying paint to' would seem to be using the word in the same sense:

> Mary painted the hall, and John, the downspouts.

Rather than say *paint* has two senses ('decorate' and 'protect') we should say that it has only one ('apply paint to') with a certain range of purposes. The intention of protecting or decorating must be present, however: if a baby wiped paint-covered hands on the wall, we would not say that it painted the wall, except ironically. Actually, one might try to apply a different sense of *paint* here—'to produce in lines and colors on a surface by putting paint on something'—but the Direct Object of *paint* for this sense must be an object of art (mural, water-color, etc.) or understood as a visual representation of the thing (*painted the tree in water-colors*—i.e., 'a picture of the tree')—presumably the baby's smears would not amount to the representation of a wall, or anything else.

For another example, consider whether *suggest* has a different sense when used with a human Subject from the sense it has when used with a nonhuman Subject:

> John suggested to Mary that she should get snow tires.
> The skid suggested to Mary that she should get snow tires.

A slight variation of the gapping test yields the mildly humorous effect of a word being used in different senses:

> John suggested to Mary that she should get snow tires and so did the skid.

Some dictionaries indicate relatedness between senses by grouping them (e.g., *Webster's New Collegiate Dictionary*, hereafter *WNC*), while others follow a linear order (*American Heritage Dictionary, Random House College Dictionary*, hereafter *AHD* and *RHCD*). Dictionaries seem to use other criteria as well as those described here in determining the number and relation of the senses of a word.

The definition of a sense of a word is the representation of the sense in terms of other words. That is, the definition **paraphrases** the sense or is **synonymous** with the word in the relevant sense (or should be). To explicate this basic notion of 'sameness of sense' it is necessary to introduce some logical terminology. Briefly, for S_1 to be said to be a paraphrase of S_2, it is necessary that S_1 and S_2 be truth-functionally equivalent (i.e., that S_1 logically entail S_2 and vice versa). Entailment is basically the notion 'follows from' and will be defined as follows:

> S_1 **entails** S_2 if, over the whole range of possible situations truly described by S_1, S_2 would be true also.

For example, the sentence:

> S_1: John got out of bed at 10 o'clock.

entails the sentence:

> S_2: John was in bed immediately prior to 10 o'clock.

because there is no situation of which S_1 would be true but S_2 false. That is, if he got out of bed at 10 o'clock, then he *necessarily* was in bed to start with. Hence the conjunction of S_1 and *not-S_2* should be a contradiction (false in all possible worlds) (the 'X' marks a contradiction):

> XJohn got out of bed at 10 o'clock though he wasn't in it then.

Other examples of entailment pairs (the arrow '→' indicates 'entails') are:

> Jumbo is an elephant. → Jumbo is a mammal.
> John stopped beating his wife. → John was beating or used to beat his wife.
> John regrets beating his wife. → John beat his wife.

(Verbs like *stop* and *regret* are called "factive" verbs because they always entail the truth of their complements.)

Some reflection is often necessary to determine whether a relation between sentences is a true logical entailment. For example, the sentence:

> S_1: He sharpened the knife.

might be said to entail:

> S_2: The knife became sharp.

There are situations, however, of which S_1 would be true but not S_2, namely ones in which the knife became less dull but still not what one would want to call sharp.

If it happens also to be the case that S_2 entails S_1, then S_1 and S_2 are logically or truth-functionally **equivalent:**

S_1: John committed suicide.
S_2: John killed himself.

S_1: Not everyone came.
S_2: Some didn't come.

Again, the relation between two sentences may be close but fall short of full equivalence. *Forbid*, for example, entails *not permit*, but there are some cases where *not permit* does not entail *forbid*—where, that is, *not permit* would be true, but *forbid* false:

They didn't permit the crabgrass to spread.

One could argue, however, that there are really two senses of *permit*, one of which is equivalent to 'grant permission to', the other equivalent to 'allow to happen', and that, for the first of these, *not permit$_1$* is equivalent to *forbid*. This still will not work, however, since the following is not a contradiction:

They didn't *permit$_1$* him to leave, but they didn't forbid him to either.

Notice, by the way, that the *suicide* example is not quite right: suppose John were an anarchist who was working on a bomb and blew himself up by mistake—in that case, S_2 would be true but not S_1. If the word *deliberately* is added to S_2, however, the sentences are equivalent.

Logical entailment must be distinguished from what might be called factual entailment. As an example of the latter, S_1 might be said to factually entail S_2:

S_1: The batter hit a fly ball into center field which was caught.
S_2: The batter was out.

The "following" of S_2 from S_1 here depends on the rules of baseball rather than the meaning of *hit a fly ball* (and of course depends on the assumption that a game was in progress). This distinction is particularly hard to draw when the factual relation is one of natural cause and effect:

S_1: It began to rain.
S_2: The ground began to get wet.

This is a factual relation, however, not a logical one, because we can imagine circumstances in which the ground would not get wet when it rained (for instance, if it were covered with a tarpaulin).

1.3

Two Aspects of
Extralogical Meaning

Sentences may convey more than their logical content. Two aspects of extralogical meaning are easily confused with logical meaning and must be distinguished from it: shadings associated with the grammatical relations Subject and Direct Object, and inferences arising from the pragmatics or "use" of sentences.

Shadings associated with what is Subject appear in the following sets:

(1)   a. John met Harry.
      b. Harry met John.
      c. John and Harry met.

(2)   a. The truck collided with the bus.
      b. The bus collided with the truck.
      c. The bus and the truck collided.

(3)   a. The car is behind the bus.
      b. The bus is in front of the car.

(4)   a. The devil used to be frightening to the ignorant.
      b. People used to be afraid of the devil before the age of science.

There seem to be three relevant properties we associate with Subjects: first, they are usually what the sentence is about (that is, the topic or **theme** under discussion). Thus (1a) seems to present the encounter as "what happened to John"—from his point of view, so to speak—but (1b) presents it from Harry's point of view and (1c) presents it as a mutual experience. So also in (3): one sentence is about the location of the car, the other about the location of the bus. Second, the Subject is often assumed to be the instigator or "doer" even when the verb does not clearly refer to an action performed by someone on someone or something. Thus in (2), (a) would be preferred if the bus were stationary, (b) if the truck were stationary, and (c) if neither were. The same considerations apply in (1) if we imagine situations where one or the other is stationary. Third, referentiality is preeminently a property of Subjects. Hence (4a) tends to suggest the existence (in at least the Speaker's mind) of a referent for *the devil* more strongly than (4b) does.

The following sets have to do with what is the Direct Object:

(5)   a. They loaded the truck with furniture.
        b. They loaded furniture onto the truck.

(6)   a. They smeared the wall with paint.
        b. They smeared paint on the wall.

(7)   a. I teach the little monsters arithmetic.
        b. I teach arithmetic to the little monsters.

(8)   a. I am angry at Mary marrying that old man.
        b. I am angry at Mary's marrying that old man.

(9)   a. I expected Mary to support me.
        b. I expected that Mary would support me.

One might say that the Direct Object is assumed to be the most directly and completely affected participant. (5a) more strongly suggests a full truck than (5b), (6a) a covered wall. (7a) suggests more strongly than (7b) success at the teaching (i.e., they learn). In (8a) and (9a) the anger and expectation seem more directed at Mary than in the (b) sentences. In none of these sets, however, is it obvious that there are different logical entailments (with the possible exception of (5) and (6), but see Exercise 12).

Certain inferences that can be made from sentences appear to be based on how the sentence functions in actual speech situations. These are generally called **conversational implicatures** to distinguish them from logical entailments. One assumes that a Speaker speaks in good faith, which means among other things that he is trying not to mislead his Hearer, is trying to convey information he thinks his Hearer wants to know or should know, and is not making unreasonable assumptions. For example, if you tell someone that something is possible, you conversationally implicate that it is not to your knowledge certain. If I said:

You may fail.

you would be justified in assuming that you have a chance to pass—such a statement from me after I had turned in an F would be highly misleading. Similarly, a Speaker who utters a simple conditional sentence:

If John did that, he will be punished.

implicates his belief that it is at least possible that John did that. If the Speaker is certain that John is innocent, he must use a counterfactual conditional:

If John had done that, he would be punished.

Conversational implicatures shade into what Jerrold Katz (1972: 428ff.) has called **presumptions**, the untruth of which also makes a sentence misleading. For example, cleft sentences normally presume that the clefted item (that which occurs between *be* and *that*) is in some way unique or contrasted to other possibilities:

> It was in the basement that they put mousetraps.

If in fact they put mousetraps all over the house, the sentence wouldn't be false, but it would be misleading in that it had led the Hearer into presuming that the mousetraps were confined to the basement. Similarly,

> Even John ran away.

presumes someone else ran away. If that is not true, the sentence is true but misleading, since one would expect

> John ran away.

or

> Only John ran away.

(the latter if some others might have run away). These matters will be taken up in more detail in the chapter on pragmatics. The purpose of mentioning them at this point is to distinguish them from the logical entailments of sentences, to which topic we now return.

1.4

Analysis into Components

The notion that the sense of a word can be expressed as a combination of the senses of other words is familiar to anyone who has used a dictionary. The goals of a semanticist and those of a lexicographer, however, differ considerably: one would like to make logical entailments and systematic relations of word senses clear, the other aims at giving clues to the common uses of words. In many cases it is possible to adapt a dictionary definition to semantic ends. For example, we can confirm the results of the gapping test with *water* by showing that the two different senses that the test indicated correspond to two different sets of entailments:

> $water_1$:   nourish by applying water to → nourish
> → put water on
>
> $water_2$:   dilute by adding water to → dilute
> → put water in

The senses of *water* here are not simply the sum of the two entailed parts, however, but include a causative or purposive relation between them. From here on, the term **component** will be used for these parts of meaning (other terms are *feature, sememe*, semantic *marker*), and they will be printed in block capitals to signify that they represent one sense of the word that they usually represent. The components may themselves abbreviate a complex of other components. There are a number of different proposals for representing the combination of components, though in fact no generally accepted one for representing the relation of an action to the purpose of it. For purposes of illustration, it is adequate to give the following analysis to *water*$_2$ in a kind of "semantic pidgin," which can easily be translated into several formal notations:

$$X \text{ WATER}_2 \ Y = X \text{ PUT WATER IN } Y \ \& \ X \text{ INTEND to DILUTE } Y$$

(where X and Y are variables standing for noun phrases and the verb is not marked for agreement with X or for tense; in the sentence *The bartender watered the drinks, X = the bartender* and *Y = the drinks*). Here PUT and DILUTE could be further analyzed.

For a second illustration, compare the definition of one sense of *give* in *AHD* to an analysis in "semantic pidgin":

'To make a present of'
X CAUSE it COME ABOUT that Y HAVE Z *(For free)*

Note that the latter analysis indicates explicitly some of the entailments of sentences with *give*, while the dictionary entry leaves these implicit in the notion of *present*. But note also that the analysis into components does not capture all of the entailments of *give*—the notion of "for free" implicit in *present* should be added.

Given an analysis into components, relatedness of meaning can easily be determined by noting the shared components. For example, *sell* can be analyzed as having all of the components of *give* except FOR FREE, and in place of that has one additional element IN-EXCHANGE-FOR-MONEY (which clearly could itself be broken down into more basic units). *Loan* could also be treated as a relative of *give* and *sell*—the distinguishing component would be WITH-PROMISE-OF-RETURN. Similarly, the relatedness and differences of *embezzle, pilfer, filch, shoplift* can be expressed by saying that they all share the components TAKE & ILLEGALLY & SURREPTITIOUSLY and that each has further components distinguishing it from the others. Again, *pursue, follow, chase* would have the components GO AFTER in common and hence would be more closely related than, say, *travel, approach*, and *rise*, which would have only the GO component in common. Equivalence arises when all of the components of one sentence are present in the other and no others:

           murder   kill deliberately

   KILL   DELIBERATELY   KILL DELIBERATELY

George A. Miller (1972) reports some research on intuitions of re-latedness of verbs of motion. Subjects were asked to sort cards with the verbs (1) *approach, visit, assemble, collect, gather,* (2) *pivot, turn, rotate, spin,* (3) *descend, fall, sink, drop, lower,* (4) *exit, leave, eject, withdraw* written in sentences of the form *He visited X* on them into piles of related words, choosing as many piles as they wished. The four groups are estab-lished on the basis of the presence of a TO, AROUND, DOWN, or OUT component, respectively, and Miller found that subjects did indeed group the cards into these four groups. This experiment, and others that Miller reports, suggest that the sort of analysis sketched here is not merely a de-scriptive convenience but does reflect something about the way speakers actually do code the senses of words.

A fairly detailed discussion of sorting and other tests of the cognitive basis of similarity judgments is given in J. M. Anglin (1970). Anglin is pri-marily concerned with the sortings performed by children of various ages compared with those performed by adults. Two conclusions bear mention here: first, children appear to make relatively less use of abstract compo-nents of similarity (e.g., CONCRETE OBJECT to group *chair* and *boy* together) than adults do and more use of "thematic relations" (*eat-apple, sugar-sweet, foot-jump, needle-doctor*); second, the fact that subjects group certain words in the way the experimenter's analysis predicts does not prove that the subjects are operating with the same analysis, only that whatever clues and tactics they are using have the same results—one can group *boy* and *chair* together because they refer to concrete objects, or because they both have legs. The perception of resemblances—or, in the case of riddles, specious resemblances—may involve information that is not coded as part of the word's meaning. Despite this important reservation, Anglin's results do suggest that learners may recode words they have already learned in more abstract terms as they mature.

The usefulness of componential analysis is perhaps most apparent when we consider the relations of words constituting an interlocking set, like kinship terms. With the components MALE, FEMALE, PARENT we can analyze the main senses of *father, mother, son, daughter, brother, sister.* For example:

> *X* is father of *Y*:   *X* PARENT *Y* & *X* MALE
> *X* is brother of *Y*: A&B PARENT *X&Y* & *X* MALE

Capturing such relations as *uncle* and *sister-in-law* introduces an extra element of complexity, since there are, as it were, two different ways to qualify for these relations—by blood:

X is uncle of Y: $A\&B$ PARENT $X\&C$ & C PARENT Y & X MALE

or by marriage:

X is uncle of Y: $A\&B$ PARENT $C\&D$ & C PARENT Y &
                       X MARRIED D & X MALE

At this point there is a decision to be made: do these constitute two different senses of *uncle*, or only one with an 'or' option involved? The dictionaries I have consulted list them as separate senses.

We have analyzed *father* in terms of a component PARENT. It should be indicated somewhere that if one is a parent, one is either a mother or a father. This could be done by "defining" *parent* as FATHER OR MOTHER. Here we confront the notorious problem of circularity in definition: we have indicated the relation of the words, but have not said anything about the criteria that must be satisfied to be a parent, nor have we given any natural account of why the MALE/FEMALE opposition occurs here—it is certainly less arbitrarily associated than with *actor/actress*. These considerations, among others, have led Anna Wierczbicka (1972) to suggest that the kinship system should take BEARING and BEGETTING as primitive terms, defining *X father of Y* as 'one who has begotten *Y*' (which, incidentally, accounts for how you can come to be, but not cease to be, a father), *male* as 'one capable of begetting' or 'possessing organs for begetting'), and *parent* as a complex term 'father or mother'. The dictionaries I have consulted are happily inconsistent, suppressing the biology of *father* but not *mother*, or the reverse. The most important moral of this discussion is that the more general term may not be cognitively more primitive, but simply the disjunction of the less general terms.

Analyzing the senses of words into components that represent the senses of other words assumes that the senses of "complex" words are represented in the mind in terms of the senses of "simpler" words. The sense of the complex word is said to be "decomposed" into components. Some linguists and psychologists have questioned whether this is in fact psychologically realistic. Fodor, Fodor, and Garrett (1975) report that certain sentences with a negatively defined word such as *bachelor* are comprehended more quickly than those with explicit negatives or even those with implicit negatives (*doubt, deny*), yet they should be of equivalent complexity if the sense of *bachelor* is decomposed into something like MALE & HUMAN & ADULT & NOT MARRIED. Since *bachelor* appears to be treated as though it is not negative, they propose that it is represented in the mind as a simple concept. The entailments of the sentence

John is a bachelor.

would be accounted for by **meaning postulates** associated with the word *bachelor* of the form:

John is a bachelor → John is not married.
                   → John is an adult.
(etc.)

They argue that if such a device is preferable in this case, then it should be the device used for all words. The essential claim is that each word is conceptually simple: the entailments of the word are a separate matter and do not reflect its conceptual structure, for indeed it has no conceptual structure as such. Walter Kintsch (1974) also came to this conclusion because he was unable to find any experimental evidence that sentences with "complex" words are harder to comprehend than those with words representing part of the meaning of the complex words (e.g., *confess/commit, accuse/guilty, convince/believe*). It is not entirely obvious, however, why *confess, accuse*, and *convince* should be measurably more difficult to comprehend than their simpler "subparts," since the "extra" components in the more complex words are among the most general around (SAY and CAUSE).

George Lakoff (1972a) points out that any semantic theory will have to make use of meaning postulates to account for entailment relations between simple ("atomic") concepts. *Certain*, for example, entails *possible*, yet *possible* does not seem in any obvious way to be part of the sense of *certain*. Lakoff's main point, however, is that this treatment should not be given to all entailments between words, or certain generalizations will be unstatable. For example, several facts about modification discussed in Chapters II (*recent American*) and IV (*sloppy typist*, also 4.2) receive a natural account if the senses of the words modified are assumed to have internal structure. (Lakoff's examples are somewhat more complex.)

The resolution of this question is not crucial for the purposes of this book. Both parties agree, after all, that knowledge of a word involves knowledge of its entailments, whether or not the entailments are always effectively in mind when we use the word. It is extremely convenient to speak of the senses of words in terms of components, and I will continue to do so; in many places the reader may read "meaning postulate" for component if he or she so wishes.

1.5

Taxonomic Hierarchies

It is not surprising that kinship terminology constitutes an interlocking set of contrasts along certain parameters. In general, terms referring to human institutions, artifacts, and actions can be defined at least roughly in this manner. The human instinct to classify and dfferentiate is most at home here—much less so in regard to natural objects and processes (e.g., *pear, thunder, wither*). There seems to be a human ability and tendency to arrange things into genera-and-species groupings, usually called **taxonomic hierarchies**, and these can be directly translated into componential definitions. For example, rifles, pistols, and shotguns can be classified as sidearms, differing in how they are held and the nature of the bore of their barrels. These contrasts can be represented in a branching tree:

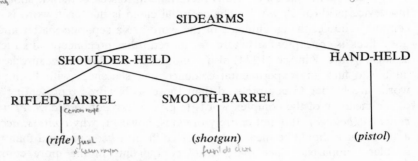

which translates into the analysis:

> *shotgun*: SIDEARM & SHOULDER-HELD & SMOOTH-BARREL
> *rifle*:   SIDEARM & SHOULDER-HELD & RIFLED-BARREL
> *pistol*: SIDEARM & HAND-HELD

Notice that the components are entailed by the words:

> It is a shotgun. → It is smooth-barreled.
>   → It is shoulder-held.
>   → It is a sidearm.

There are other attributes of shotguns, however, not represented in the definition. These would include: PELLET-FIRING, DOUBLE-BARREL, SHORT RANGE, and FOR SHOOTING GAME. These attributes differ from the preceding ones, however, in that they are not necessary properties of things called shotguns. That is, they are not entailed by the sentence *It is a shotgun*; rather, they are only **associated** components. The phrase *rifled shotgun* is contradictory: there can be no object properly called a shotgun that is rifled. The phrases *slug-firing shotgun, single-barreled shotgun*, and so on are not contradictory: the modifiers block off components that are only associated.

Dictionaries do not always clearly distinguish between associated and **definitional** components in their definitions. In some respects this is wise, because people do not organize their hierarchies in exactly the same way, but lexicographers sometimes give way to the impulse to write a brief essay on the thing being defined. Compare the definitions of *shotgun* from three major current dictionaries:

> (*AHD*)   A shoulder-held firearm that fires multiple pellets through a smooth bore.
>
> (*WNC*)   An often double-barreled smoothbore shoulder weapon for firing shot at short ranges.
>
> (*RHCD*) A smoothbore gun for firing small shot to kill birds and small quadrupeds, though often used with buckshot to kill larger animals.

It seems that the *RHCD* has, perhaps unintentionally, gone from telling us how to use the word *shotgun* to telling us how shotguns are used in our culture (why is 'riot-control' not included?). Nonetheless, some associated elements would seem to be part of the meaning of the word in the looser sense of *meaning* as 'what people think of when they hear/speak the word', though not part of the definitional core that yields logical entailments and contradictions.

For a second example, consider the field of "writing instruments" which could be arranged in a hierarchy so:

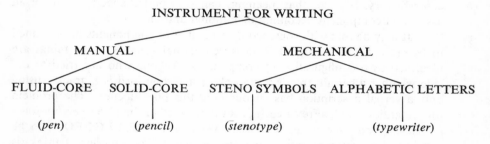

Then the definition of *pen* and *pencil* can be given as

> *pen:*   INSTRUMENT FOR WRITING & HAND-HELD & FLUID-CORE
>
> *pencil:* INSTRUMENT FOR WRITING & HAND-HELD & SOLID-CORE

There would seem to be some associated components with *pen*, one of which might be HAVING METAL NIB, and with *pencil* also, perhaps CORE OF GRAPHITE and ERASABLE. These components are usually only associated, since they can be blocked off by a modifier without giving a contradictory phrase:

> ball-point pen
> felt-tip pen

grease pencil
indelible pencil

Suppose, however, some persons had the hierarchy differently constructed
so that the component distinguishing pens from pencils was not FLUID/
SOLID but ERASABLE/NOT ERASABLE:

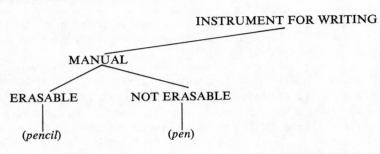

These persons would presumably have FLUID CORE as an associated
component for *pen*, SOLID CORE for *pencil*. They then would find nothing
contradictory in the phrase *liquid pencil* (where the first person would find
a flatly contradictory reading) but would find the phrase *indelible pencil*
contradictory. It seems that meanings can vary and change in terms of an
associated component becoming definitional and vice versa.

It may be that with some words a number of components are assumed
to be present, but no one of them is definitional—that is, some things are
identified by a configuration of components. Anyone who has tried to decide whether a certain tree is a pin oak or a certain bird is a grackle using
only a verbal description has encountered this phenomenon. The problem
for semantics, as Geoffrey Leech poses it, is whether the phrase *eighty-four-
legged elephant* is contradictory (i.e., whether FOUR-LEGGED is to be
considered definitional with respect to *elephant*). The problem, I think, is
that it is hard to imagine how an eighty-four-legged creature could have
the general "morph" of an elephant. If it were to have it, and all of the
other characteristics of an elephant, we might agree to call it an eighty-four-
legged elephant. This problem will receive further attention in the following
chapter.

1.6

More on Associated Components

Speakers not only discriminate definitional and associated components—
they discriminate between closely and loosely associated components.
George Lakoff (1972b) has pointed out that hedge-words like *technically,*

What is a hedge-word?

strictly, loosely speaking, sort of, kind of, regular, and *real* are sensitive to these discriminations. There are things that, while possessing the definitional attributes necessary to be referred to by an item, lack any of the associated attributes. In this case the hedge-word *technically* is appropriate:

> Mae West is technically a spinster.   *vieille fille*

If the definitional attributes are present, and also some closely associated one or ones, but the more loosely associated ones are absent, the likely hedge-word is *strictly speaking*:

> Strictly speaking, a whale is a mammal.

If we still want to refer to something that lacks the definitional attributes but has some of the associated ones, we can use *loosely speaking* or *in a manner of speaking*:

> Loosely speaking, the whale is a fish.
> In a manner of speaking, bats are birds.   *Façon de parler, les chauves-souris sont des oiseaux*

Finally, if something has some attribute only loosely associated, and lacks the definitional and more tightly associated ones, the appropriate hedge is *real* or *regular*:

> Harry is a regular fish.
> Sam is a real tiger.

Notice that in the last examples the hedge-word can be omitted. This reflects the establishment of **extended senses** for *fish* and *tiger*: an associated component of one sense has become the basis of a distinct sense. Since the sense is based on a component only associated with the first sense, it is not surprising that dictionaries differ remarkably in their definitions of these extended senses. Compare these definitions of an extended sense of *tiger*:

(AHD)	*3.*	a fierce, aggressive, or audacious person.
(RHCD)	*3.*	an especially energetic, dynamic, or hard-working person.
(WNC)	*2a.*	a fierce and bloodthirsty person or quality.
(SOED)	*4.*	*transf. & fig.* Applied to one who or that which in some way resembles or suggests a tiger.

Note that *SOED (Shorter Oxford English Dictionary)* avoids specifying which attributes are carried over when *tiger* is "applied"—the use of *transf*-(erred) and *fig*(urative) here is typical of the *OED*.

A second very common type of extended sense is one that is less specified than the base: the effect seems often to be a shift up on the taxonomic hierarchy or the toleration of usage when some definitional and/or primary criterion is missing. In regard to *tiger*,

(*AHD*)   2. Broadly, any of various other similar felines.

Sun and *moon* similarly mean "our" sun and moon or "any such."

Dictionaries frequently distinguish between what can be called the "broad" use of a word and its "narrower" use in terms of "sense-dividers" such as *specif*(ically) and *esp*(ecially):

> (*WNC*)   *knife*$_{vt}$: to use a knife on; *specif.* to stab, slash, or wound with a knife.

Similarly, the definition given for *university* recognizes a broader and narrower usage:

> *university*: an institution of higher learning providing facilities for teaching and research and authorized to grant academic degrees; *specif.*:   one made up of an undergraduate division which confers bachelor's degrees and a graduate division which comprises a graduate school and professional schools each of which may confer master's degrees and doctorates (*WNC*).

(*AHD*, by the way, does not recognize the "broader" usage for *university*.) The sense-dividers *often* and *usu*(ally) appear to separate definitional from associated elements:

> VICE — usspelling
> (*WNC*)   *vise*$_n$: any of various tools with two jaws for holding work that close usu. by a screw, lever, or cam.

Here clearly the means of closing the jaws is not a definitional part of a vise.

Parallel to the attributes associated with nouns are components of manner, purpose, or instrument associated with, or definitionally a part of, the meanings of verbs. As noted above, an element of purpose is definitionally a part of the verb *paint*, namely to protect or decorate, and similarly for *water*. In fact, the senses of *water* may be said to be distinguished by the respective purposes of 'putting water in/on'. With instruments, however, the situation is somewhat different: these tend to be associated, since

> slice with a wire
> bake on the coals
> shoot with a bow and arrow

are not contradictory, though knives, ovens, and guns are the normally associated instruments. In regard to manner adverbials, *enamel* and *measure* are usually thought of as done *carefully*, but not necessarily; similarly, *kill* is usually thought of as done with some violence, so that

> kill gently/softly

is striking and unexpected, but not contradictory.

Sometimes the only components distinguishing the meanings of verbs are associated components. Dictionaries agree that *hint, suggest,* and a few others have as definitional components IMPART THOUGHTS OR IDEAS INDIRECTLY (that is, *suggest*$_1$ does). Here the manner component INDI-RECTLY is definitional. Dictionaries distinguish the words by the asso-ciated degree of indirectness, but, not surprisingly in view of what has been said concerning associated components, they differ:

(*WNC*)   *hint* implies the use of slight or remote suggestion with a min-
          imum of overt statement.
(*AHD*)   *hint* refers to expression that is indirect but contains rather
          pointed clues.

If synonymy is defined as identity of ALL components, definitional and asso-ciated, then *hint* and *suggest* are not synonymous, though they are logically equivalent. So defined, synonymy turns out to be very rare. The reason it is rare seems to be that as learners, we assume users are making distinctions when they use different words, though we may have great difficulty grasping them. Most people who are familiar with the terms differentiate *couch* and *sofa, antenna* and *aerial* by means of some associated components, though there is considerable variation with regard to which ones.

1.7

How Children Learn
Word Meanings

It is well known that younger children appear to overgeneralize the first words they learn, applying them to a wider range of things than they would be applied to in adult speech. A number of people, including Eve Clark (1973), have pointed out that these overgeneralizations can be viewed as underspecified senses. For example, if certain children use *apple* to refer to oranges, tennis balls, door knobs, and paper weights as well as apples, one can conclude from their uses that they have for the sense of *apple* [SPHERICAL & SMALL] and not much else. Their learning to restrict the term to the range of things that adults call apples would involve adding definitional components to that sense, and perhaps in some cases demoting a component previously taken as definitional to associated status, or drop-ping an associated component altogether. Demotion appears to be involved in children's learning of kinship terms, where the component ADULT seems definitional for *uncle* for younger children but of course must be demoted to associated status to get an adult's sense of *uncle*.

There is a fairly good basis (surveyed in Clark, 1973) for supposing that the components children initially make use of for definitions are those that refer to perceivable qualities like shape, sound, and texture rather than those that refer to more abstract properties like function (what something is used for). Since, for very many nouns, what it is used for, or functions as, is important in its definition, children will have to considerably reorganize their vocabularies as they come to recognize that at times a functional definition, rather than a physical one, gives a more coherent generalization about the things people call, e.g., *polish*. Some research by Elaine Andersen (1975) concerning the terms *cup* and *glass* explores the specification that children of different ages have of these terms by asking them to name and sort an array of objects as cups, glasses, or neither. Not all of the objects would be called either glass or cup by adults (i.e., there are some glass bowl-like things in the array). The observer can infer the bases of the naming and the specificity of the terms. It appears that younger children (up to six years) take the physical shape and material as the predominant definitional components, the older ones, like adults, rely more on probable function. Thus younger children will call a tall cylindrical plastic container a cup because it is made of plastic, especially if colored plastic, and a glass "bowl" a glass. There is a great deal more to be learned from this study, which the reader is urged to consult.

These terms are particularly tricky, because one term is also the name of a material (*glass*) but *cup* is not. This seems to induce us to call a thing that is a glass in shape and function a paper cup, though it may lack a handle. Having a handle is in general a good discriminator of a cup, but not perfect, and there are mugs to worry about as well as small bowls. In short, these terms "partition" the field of "drinking vessels" (notice the functionally defined term *drinking* has been smuggled in) but they do not constitute a discrete partitioning of the field—there are overlaps and conflicting criteria—and a taxonomic hierarchy like that set up for sidearms would be very difficult to construct. This situation is not uncommon: Adrienne Lehrer (1969) has noted that the set of verbs of cooking is not perfectly analyzable into a single hierarchy (*roast*, for example, overlaps *bake* and *broil*), and one might find similar results for *pot/pan*, etc. (and see Lehrer, 1974). Older children and adults come to accept that the most natural and useful senses of terms may be neither inclusive enough to refer appropriately to any object we come across or conclusive enough to decide whether a given thing should be called by one or another term (consider *anxiety, fear, apprehension, uneasiness*, . . .). They learn to modify and hedge their applications and even to explain them: "You could call it a cup since it is cuppy in shape—bowls are wider and shallower"; "It's sort of a bowl"; and so on.

The shift that Andersen found from components based on form (in the broad sense of 'all physical characteristics') to those of function is most interesting in regard to adult definitions of instrument and artifact nouns generally. Dictionary definitions often mention both form and function, sometimes giving more weight to form, sometimes to function. Consider the definitions of *hammer* and *polish* given in *WNC*:

> *hammer*$_n$: *1a.* A hand tool consisting of a solid head set crosswise on a handle and used for pounding.
>
> *polish*$_n$: *3.* A preparation that is used to produce a gloss and often a color for the protection and decoration of a surface.

Form and function are given about equal weight for *hammer*, but with *polish* function is the sole component. If children's definitions are heavy to the form side and weak to the function, one would expect them to generalize *hammer* to include axes and adzes and to have some trouble getting a stable sense for *polish*. I noticed both phenomena in my daughter's speech at age three, who insisted on calling shoe polish, applied with a brush, *paint*, but rejected the term for an unpigmented polish squeezed from a tube and applied with a rag, suggesting with question intonation: toof-paste?! I do not know the degree to which adults vary in the amount of redefinition they have performed for individual words and the relative weight they give to form and function, but I suspect that it may be fairly great. Georgia Green (1972: 86) observed that for her "anything which could be used to paste with is paste, but not everything that you could 'glue' with is glue." For me, it is roughly the opposite: *glue* is the more functionally defined term, *paste* the more formally defined.

There is an apparent contradiction between the claimed priority of formal to functional definition and recent work by Katherine Nelson (1974) discussed by Judith Kornfeld (1975), though this turns on what is meant by *function*. Nelson argues that very young children (12 to 15 months) appear to class items as similar that can be acted upon in the same way: they will, for example, pick a cylinder as 'like a ball' rather than a fixed sphere held in a frame because they can roll the cylinder but not the fixed sphere. This is a dynamic or "motor"-oriented classification, which may be reanalyzed in terms of "static" properties of form later. Obviously, *function* as we have been using the term is a far more abstract kind of coding involving typical or canonical or intended uses. Kornfeld reports cases of retarded and learning-disabled children (mental age two and a half to four years) who seem still to be functioning on this level, responding to a direction to "put the book on the chair" by taking the book and sitting on the chair. In effect, *chair* seems to be coded 'for sitting on' whenever it turns up. Nelson observes that this sort of primitive, preconceptual "knowledge" of things (and relations) is important even in adulthood.

A final point is that functional properties are inherently relational, while form properties are not, and that words that involve relational components in their definitions (e.g., kinship terms, many adjectives) are not mastered in the exact adult sense until quite late in childhood (9 to 11 years). This suggests that relational components involve greater cognitive complexity than formal components. The reanalysis of, e.g., *X brother Y* from [*X* MALE & *X* NOT ADULT] to [*X* MALE & *A&B* PARENT *X&Y*] is not merely the substitution of one definitional component for another: it is the substitution of a relational for a nonrelational one and as such reflects a major step in cognitive development.

When learners acquire a new word, they may or may not adjust the meanings of related words they have already learned. One might think of the process of adjustment as parallel to the difference in the definitions of *telescope* in *SOED* (1933) and in *AHD* (1969):

> (*SOED*) An optical instrument for making distant objects appear nearer and larger, consisting of one or more tubes with an arrangement of lenses. . . .
>
> (*AHD*) An instrument for collecting and examining electromagnetic radiation, especially 1. an arrangement of lenses or mirrors. . . .

The practice of referring to a new contrivance as a *radio telescope* (rather than, say, a *telescopic radio*) has led *AHD* to broaden the main sense, treating the components having to do with optics as 'narrowers' or 'specifiers'. The result is a change in type of definition from form + function to function alone.

This chapter has been about the structure of word senses. Analyzing the senses of words into configurations of components enables one to predict for a given sentence what its entailments will be, what other sentences will be equivalent to it, what sentences will be redundant, and what contradictory. These components constitute the definitional core of a sense. Other components appear to be present also, though not so centrally as to effect the truth-value of sentences containing the word. Speakers vary somewhat in their sorting of components into definitional, closely and loosely associated groups, and some of the variation may be a residue of incomplete reanalysis of previously learned senses.

The judgments not yet discussed are those of ambiguity and anomaly. The meanings of words are also reflected in the potential of the word for combining with other words. One of the things that speakers know about *amuse*, for example, is that it requires the noun that functions as its Direct Object to refer to a thing of a certain class, namely, a human or animal. Otherwise the sentence will be anomalous (*They amused the tulips.*). This is called a **selectional** (or **co-occurrence**) **restriction** of the verb *amuse*. The operation of selectional restrictions is reflected in the fact that words are generally more determinate in meaning when used in sentences than when cited in isolation. The word *water*, in isolation, might be thought of as a noun or a verb. In

> She watered them.

it is clearly a verb because of its construction with a noun and a pronoun, but it is still ambiguous over at least two senses. But if the Direct Object is further specified:

> She watered the plants.

the possibility of the 'dilute' sense is cancelled. How the sense of a word interacts with the other words in construction with it will be the topic of the next chapter.

READINGS FOR CHAPTER I

For general discussion of the domain of semantics, see Katz (1972), Fillmore (1969), Leech (1969, 1974), and Moravcsik (1972). Bierwisch (1970) is a concise introduction to basic concepts.

Zwicky and Sadock (1973) is the most complete discussion of ambiguity tests to date. Bolinger (1965) is the source for some of the discussion of dictionary definition. Chapters 9 and 10 of Lyons (1968) are sound surveys of theories of meaning, basic distinctions, and componential analysis.

Labov (1973) argues that criteria based on form and those based on function may interact. If asked to imagine utensils with various degrees of resemblance to a cup holding coffee, subjects will call more of them cups than if asked to imagine them holding mashed potatoes.

Smith et al. (1974) and Rips et al. (1975) report experiments bearing on relatedness of meaning. They found, for instance, that false sentences with words of related meaning (*A carrot is a fruit. Oaks have cylindrical leaves.*) are not recognized to be false as quickly as sentences with words of less related meanings (*A car is a fruit. Oaks have fragile glasses.*).

Factive verbs and adjectives have been studied by many following the lead of Kiparsky and Kiparsky (1971) and Karttunen (1971, 1971a). These writers claim that factives presuppose their complements, but Kempson (1975) and Wilson (1972) argue that this is simply an entailment relation. Karttunen has also discussed other similar classes of verbs, which he calls semi-factives and neg-factives.

Katz and Nagel (1974) argue against using meaning postulates in semantic representation. Bartsch and Vennemann (1972) declare for them, though they misunderstand Lakoff's arguments.

Nida (1975, especially chapters 3 and 4) is a more detailed account of partitioning of semantic fields and of related senses of single words. His distinction of diagnostic/supplementary components is not, however, the same as our definitional/associated.

Componential analysis has been developed by anthropologists as well as linguists. See Tyler (1969) for a representative group of articles.

EXERCISES AND PROBLEMS

1. Explain the "puns" in
   He gave the house a coat of paint and his wife one of suede.
   W. C. Fields was a real fish and so is Mark Spitz.

2. What logical relation do (a) and (b) stand in?
   (a) John read journals until 10 o'clock. $a \rightarrow b$
   (b) John read journals before 10 o'clock. $b \nrightarrow a$

3. All of the following fall short of being logically equivalent. Describe a situation of which one would be true and not the other.
   (1) A = He has forgotten where his friend lives.
   (2) A = He brought John to the party.
       B = He caused John to come to the party.
   (3) A = He knows how to swim.
       B = He has ceased to know where his friend lives.
       B = He can swim.

4. Which of the following are logically equivalent? For those you reject, describe a situation (as before):
   (1) A = He didn't remain in the room.
       B = He left the room.
       (given that: he was in the room)
   (2) A = John is taller than Harry.
       B = Harry is shorter than John.
   (3) A = They thinned the paint.
       B = They caused the paint to become thin.

5. How do *steal* and *rob* relate to *embezzle, pilfer*, etc. in terms of components? Is *steal* closer to *embezzle/pilfer*, or is *rob* closer?

6. Construct a componential analysis for *sister-in-law* using the components PARENT, MARRIED, and FEMALE.

7. Explain what is strange about: an indelible liquid pencil.

8. How is the notion of redundancy defined in terms of components?

9. Explain what is odd or false about:
   (a) Strictly speaking, the President is the chief executive.
   (b) A beagle is sort of a dog.
   (c) Loosely speaking, Peter is a skunk.
   (d) A whale is a typical mammal.
   (e) Strictly speaking, tomatoes are vegetables.

10. Look up *panther* and *leopard* in a dictionary and discuss whether they should be regarded as synonymous.

11. Charles Fillmore has observed that a gun need not look like a gun, but an "imitation gun" must. Discuss this in regard to definitional and associated components.

12. An alternative to the discussion of *load* and *smear* given in the text is to view them as having two different senses in the examples and to deny the logical equivalence (so Fillmore, 1970/71). Discuss your intuitions concerning whether *load truck with furniture* entails *fill truck by loading furniture onto it*.

13. Construct a taxonomic hierarchy for *liquefy, melt, condense, deliquesce.*

14. Are the following logically equivalent? Paraphrases?
    (a) John killed Harry.
    (b) John brought it about that Harry died.

15. Are *deprive/spare, abnormal/unusual* sets of synonyms? Are they logically equivalent?

Decontextualization

Decontextualization is the term Dwight Bolinger (1965) used to describe how word meanings are learned. The notion in the broadest terms is that one can get the gist of what he hears or reads even though that may include unfamiliar words. One can match up parts of meaning with individual words and arrive at a conjecture about the meaning of the unfamiliar word. The word meaning is decontextualized in that the word is assumed to carry it outside of the context of its use. One can file it away, try to use it, and revise it as further contexts may induce one to. By context is meant either verbal context or referential context—i.e., the actual scene that is being described. This chapter will concentrate on verbal context, but, as will quickly appear, imagined referential context is always lurking around. (The discussion in this and the next chapter is greatly simplified by the assumption that the learner is able to segment utterances into words and parts of words. For some discussion of how learners develop this ability to segment, see Roger Brown (1973: 390–99), where some interesting work in artificial intelligence is touched on.)

2.1

Decontextualization from Verbal Contexts

American readers of British mystery stories frequently encounter terms unfamiliar to them, such as *spanner*, or else other terms that do not "make sense" if they are assumed to bear any of senses the reader has coded for them (*lift*), though sometimes the incongruity is apparent only in certain contexts (*vacation*). Most readers probably do not rush for a dictionary the first time they encounter the word *spanner*. Instead, they infer as much as they can about the probable sort of object referred to and wait for further contexts to check the hypothesis. If the readers' first encounter with the term is in some sentence such as

He seems to have died from a blow of a spanner or other blunt object.

they can infer not only that a spanner is a blunt object but, in the context of a murder mystery, probably also the sort of thing one could wield as an instrument. If a few pages later he read:

The Inspector noticed the chauffeur changing a tyre with a shiny spanner.

the only new purely linguistic information is 'can be used to change tires', but they can draw on their knowledge of tire-changing to add that it would either be a jacking device or some sort of wrench or tire-iron. A further context, say:

. . . tightening the nuts with a spanner . . .

would suffice to eliminate the 'jack' possibility, so, on the assumption that *spanner* is being used in the same sense in all three instances (and there is no reason to suspect otherwise), our readers can give as a definition: 'A blunt instrument used for tightening nuts (and changing tires)', or in terms of objects they are familiar with, what would be called either a wrench or a tire-iron.

   This process of matching part of the total meaning to the word is captured by what Martin Joos (1972) calls "semantic axiom number one." Roughly paraphrased, this is: "Assume that the word adds the least amount of meaning consistent with the contexts of its use." On first reading, this seems wildly counterintuitive—isn't it the function of words to add meaning to what is already there?—but in practice it is the only reasonable way for readers, or lexicographers, to proceed.

   For a second example, consider the situation of readers beginning to read *The Faerie Queene* in an unannotated edition. At the end of the second stanza they encounter the following lines describing a knight:

> Right faithful true he was in deede and word,
> But of his cheere did seeme too solemne sad,
> Yet nothing did he dread, but ever was ydrad.

How can they guess the meaning of *ydrad*? Two paths are open and should give compatible results: the first begins with the opposition marked by *but*: *ydrad* must be contrasted to dreading—hence one might suppose something like 'brave'. The structure of the word *ydrad*, however, gives a clue—to those familiar with earlier English—to a slightly better analysis. (See Chapter III, especially Exercise 5.)

The next example shows a limit of "axiom one." Suppose some individuals learning to cook from a cookbook read the instruction to scald a duck in a pot of boiling water, and later they come across a warning in the instructions for making cocoa not to scald the milk. If they assume that *scald* has the same sense in both uses, the best they can infer will be 'boil' and they may ruin the cocoa, since milk will scald before it boils. Similarly, readers coming across the following sentence in a murder mystery:

> They took the lift to the third floor.

may consider modifying one of the senses of *lift* they already have to include the sense that *lift* has here, but they doubtless will eventually conclude that it is best to leave them unmodified and postulate a new sense, which, it will turn out, occurs in just the contexts where they would use the term *elevator*. The psychological process whereby a reader calculates that an unfamiliar sense is probably operative (as opposed to the stretching of a familiar one) is an interesting and, as far as I know, little investigated one.

Thus far it has been assumed that decontextualization absolutely detaches the sense from the contexts in which it occurs. This is radically false, as the following sentences show:

(1)   The building was erected by June first.
(2)   The building was erected by the site of the new supermarket.
(3)   The building was erected by the Cosmic Construction Company.
(4)   The liturgy must be learned by heart.

Here four different senses of *by* must be postulated. The first two are close, but the first carries an entailment ('on or before') that the second does not. If the four senses were possible without regard to context, each sentence should be four ways ambiguous. Plainly this is not the case: each sense is possible only for a certain range of objects. For the first three sentences, though not for the fourth, general characterizations of the classes of objects can be given: the first sense is possible with (or selected by) an object understood to refer to a point in time, the second with an object taken to refer to a location, and the third with an object taken to refer to some animate

entity (a usual extension with nouns referring to a group of animate entities). It is possible to read (3) as if it were like (2) by viewing *Cosmic Construction Company* as standing for 'the office (building) of CCC'—hence
(3) can be said to be ambiguous over two readings. When there are *no*
senses of the words that can be matched to give a congruent reading, the
construction is anomalous:

(5)   ?The building was erected by the migration habits of the swallow.

The general point is that decontextualization can proceed only so far: some
notation must be made of the range of contexts in which that sense can
occur. This notation for by_1 would amount to 'has this sense only if object
refers to something which can be viewed as marking a point in time'. In
the Katz-Fodor (1963) notation these selectional components (the ones
that tell when the sense can operate) are enclosed in angled brackets to
distinguish them from the definitional components, which are enclosed in
square brackets. Thus:

by_1 *X*: [AT OR BEFORE *X*] ⟨*X* TIME⟩

It is not claimed that every expression that occurs in *X* has a definitional
component TIME, but only that the X can be taken as referring to a point
in time. Any noun referring to an event, for example, could occur:

(1′)   They erected the building by the election.

and it is just this set of nouns that can occur as Subject of _____ *is on Mon-
day*. The practical device of dictionaries is to use words in the paraphrase
that have the same selectional restriction. Thus by_1 is usually defined as
'not later than', where *later than* also selects a point-time expression.

It should be evident that the phenomena of sense-selection and
anomaly, when and insofar as they can be formulated in terms of general
classes, reflect components of meaning, though they may be only associated
or associable components. General statements of the relevant classes of
times can be given for by_1, by_2, and by_3, but the class of objects that selects
(is congruent with) by_4 has very few members (*heart*, ?*rote*)—and even they
do not have any of their usual senses, but a special one that occurs only in
combination with by_4. Thus it is an **idiom** by Uriel Weinreich's definition
(1966, 1969). There is no general statement about the class of items that
select the fourth sense of *by*.

English has a rich variety of partitive terms, among them the italicized
words, and a rule for which word to use with which item can sometimes be
given in terms of a general component, sometimes not:

sheet of paper/glass/plywood . . .
drop of blood/alcohol/gasoline . . .
bar of chocolate/gold/soap . . .
stick of candy/incense/wax/dynamite/gum . . .
blade of grass

Sheet is unrestricted with respect to its "objects." The class of possible objects of *drop* can be characterized by the component LIQUID (which must be understood as a possible modifier of the object, possibly redundant), but it teases the mind to characterize the *stick of* class versus the *bar of* class. With *blade of* there is clearly no generalization to be made, since *blade* occurs in partitive construction only with *grass* (or other grasslike things). It has, moreover, a sense unique to this construction, or virtually unique, so that *blade of grass* is a kind of idiom, but only a **semi-idiom,** since *grass* retains its usual sense. (Other semi-idioms are *white lie, hard liquor, hard water, hardwood*, and perhaps *hard money*, though with the last, a few other terms are possible (e.g., *cash*), so *AHD* simply notes 'said of money' for this sense of *hard* and doesn't list *hard money* as a (semi)idiom.)

2.2

Selectional Restrictions with Nouns

In most treatments of selectional restriction, a small set of components is enumerated, which, it is assumed, represent clear and distinct concepts that are attached to various words and are mentioned in the selectional restrictions of the senses of other words, so that a "match" activates the sense as a possible reading and "no match" over any sense of the words results in anomaly (i.e., no reading for composite construction). In this section I will discuss the terms *mass, concrete*, and *animate* in more than usual detail, because it seems far from certain that these represent quite the simple, primary concepts they are often assumed to.

The first selectional feature to be considered is the most debatable, some claiming that there is no semantic generalization to be made (i.e., no semantic component as such involved—Katz, 1972), others that there is. Consider the following table, where the nouns (or senses of nouns) that are compatible with *much/less/little* are listed in the left column, those with *many* and *few* in the right:

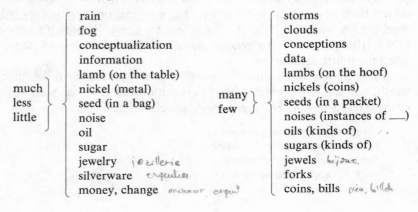

	rain		storms
	fog		clouds
	conceptualization		conceptions
	information		data
much	lamb (on the table)		lambs (on the hoof)
less	nickel (metal)	many	nickels (coins)
little	seed (in a bag)	few	seeds (in a packet)
	noise		noises (instances of __)
	oil		oils (kinds of)
	sugar		sugars (kinds of)
	jewelry ʲᵒᵗⁱˡˡᵉʳⁱᵉ		jewels ᵇⁱʲᵒᵘˣ
	silverware ᶜʳᵖᵘˡⁱᵉⁱ		forks
	money, change ᵐⁱⁿⁿᵘˢ ᵃʳᵖᵘⁱ		coins, bills ᵖⁱᵉᵃ, ᵇⁱˡˡˢ

The nouns in the second column are said to be COUNT nouns, those in the first column nonCOUNT or MASS nouns. The table is set up to suggest the difficulties involved in claiming that there is one obvious, constant property that the nouns in one column share but the others lack. Clearly 'individuated' would be a plausible approximation, but it would be hard to predict from the look of knives, forks, and spoons that *silverware* is a MASS noun, a stack of sheets of paper is *paper*, but a stack of photographs is *pictures*. If MASS or COUNT were based on some perceptual given, we would expect words that translate these in other languages to show the same differentiation, and this they manifestly do not do (see Quirk et al., 1972: 130). It certainly seems arbitrary that there is a MASS term for a pile of coins (*change*) but not for a wad of bills (*money* being too broad—the closest I can come is *folding money*). *lisac vs monnaie (papier monnaie)*

On the other hand, many have held that accompanying the choice of quantifier is some element of meaning that, if not definable in terms of independently justified physical or perceptual properties of the referents of the nouns, is at least associated with them because of their preference for one set of quantifiers or the other. It has often been observed that children seek a semantic rationale for syntactic properties. Suppose children were to try to code and predict the mass/count classification of a noun on the basis of the look of its referents. They would then produce things like *too many silverwares* and *not very many moneys* (= 'folding money'). Subsequently they would learn *silverware* and *money* as exceptions to the semantic strategy, but they might retain the semantic coding for the ones it did work with. There is enough regularity in the language on this point that they would not have to abandon the component INDIVIDUATED as fruitless.

Many if not most adjectives are commonly said to have both concrete and abstract senses. This distinction applies as much to the nouns they modify in that the "concrete" sense of an adjective selects a "concrete" sense of the noun (and/or vice versa). *Concrete* is not the most happily chosen word—some writers prefer *physical object* (= 'anything that can be perceived by one or more of the senses')—but we will stick with it. Note, by the way, that the verbs *see* and *feel* (etc.) can be said to have concrete or abstract senses depending on whether their Direct Objects are understood to be concrete or not:

I felt her pulse.
I felt her hostility.

There is little doubt that some such category as "physical object" is perceptually grounded and available for use in generalizing selectional restrictions, but in fact it is often too general to state the facts precisely. For example, while it is true that *hard* can only have the sense that it does in *hard cushion* with nouns referring to CONCRETE entities, it will not have that sense with all CONCRETE objects (?*hard cloud,* ?*hard puddle,* ?*hard wool*, *?hard picture*)—the property involved is the more specific one of having a resisting surface (roughly the same set of things that can be *pierced*). Further, CONCRETE is sometimes too broad to discriminate senses—there is more than one "physical" or "concrete" sense for *hard* (*hard steel*). This problem is even greater for *thin* (*thin wall*, *thin soup*, *thin boy*, *thin light*). As a general cover term, CONCRETE is useful, but it is probably only rarely mentioned in actual selectional restrictions.

Animate is another cover-term that seems to embrace two or three distinguishable properties usually shared by most entities, or believed to be shared, but not obviously parts of the same concept. The first property is that of capacity for locomotion and action:

> The feather rose.
> The old man rose.

The second sentence is ambiguous over two readings, the first of which is the sense 'go up', which occurs with *feather*, the second of which is the 'get up' sense, which can operate only when the Subject is understood capable of locomotion. The next pair illustrate this difference for 'action':

> Those flowers reminded me of my mother's funeral.
> She reminded me of my mother's funeral.

Again, the second sentence is ambiguous over one sense of *remind* ('trigger into consciousness') that is possible in the first sentence also and one ('put in mind') that is possible only with Subjects capable of performing actions. (Wallace Chafe [1970] calls this property *potency* and treats it as distinct from, but entailed by, animacy.)

The second property usually linked to animacy is the capacity for sensation and perception:

> The car felt hot.
> The boy felt hot.

Again, the second has an extra sense that is possible only when the Subject of *feel* is viewed as capable of experiencing sensation.

The third property is the capacity to feel emotion:

angry blister	inflamed the wound	cold car
angry boy	inflamed the crowd	cold boyfriend

Here the senses differ depending on the animacy/inanimacy of the referent of the noun. One may scruple, however, at attributing the full range of affects and desires to, say, snakes or snails. Similarly, *thinks* and a few other cogitation verbs and adjectives (*stupid*, *smart*) are used of some animals with little sense of impropriety, but probably not all would be. This would seem to depend on one's view of the psyche of the animal in question.

Notice that while these properties "go together" in the world as we experience it, and usually cohere with CONCRETE as well, the only obviously necessary connection is between LOCOMOTION and CONCRETE. Science-fiction writers can speak of entities that feel or cogitate without being embodied. The sense of cohesion among these properties is strong, however, and underlies the medieval notion of the 'animal soul'.

The temporal adjectives have an interesting property when modifying nationality terms. Most dictionaries give two senses ('citizenship' and 'native land') for nationality terms such as *American, Austrian*, etc. A sentence like

He is an American.

would then be ambiguous, though

He is a $\left\{\begin{array}{l}\text{former}\\\text{ex-}\\\text{recent}\\\text{new}\end{array}\right\}$ American.

can refer only to citizenship, not native land. We could invent a component, say 'CONTINGENT', that would be associated with the 'citizen' senses of these terms only and would be mentioned as a selectional requirement of *former, recent,* etc. It may not be necessary to do this, however, if we define the 'native' sense as 'one who was born in *N*' and take it as trivial that this 'historical fact" cannot cease to be or come to be the case (except by birth), so the modifiers would not apply. They would, however, apply to the tensable element of the sense 'one who *is* a citizen of *N*', indicating in the case of *ex-* or *former* that this identifying property no longer holds of the referent at the time of utterance. The importance of this phenomenon is that it shows the meaning of nouns can involve relations in time, not simply timeless, inherent properties of things.

2.3

Selectional Restrictions with Verbs

In this section I will again discuss general and widely used concepts—'action' and 'change-of-state'—and it will quickly emerge that these concepts are a great deal murkier than those associated with nouns. This obscurity may reflect the global nature of 'events' and 'actions'—one is less certain of the properties belonging to the verb per se than of the properties belonging to the noun.

A large number of verbs in English have senses that characterize the

Contingency: SG probable or possible but uncertain of occurrence
(He contingencies of history are unpredictable)

Subject as performing an **action** and senses in which this is not the case. In each of the sets below, the (a) sentences are unambiguously nonaction, the (c) sentences unambiguously action, and the (b) sentences ambiguous over nonaction and action senses of the verb:

(1)   a. The antimacassar stood on a picnic table.
        b. She stood where no one could see her.
        c. John stood boldly on a picnic table.
            John stood on a picnic table and made a speech.

(2)   a. The ball hit the barn with a thud.
            John hit the barn with a thud.
        b. John hit Bill's car.
        c. John hit the barn energetically.
            John hit the barn with a hammer.

(3)   a. The doctor felt her ankle rubbing his.
        b. He felt her ankle.
        c. The doctor felt her ankle carefully.

(4)   a. The flowers reminded him of his mother's funeral.
        b. His secretary reminded him of his mother's funeral.
        c. His secretary reminded him tactfully of his mother's funeral.

We have already seen why (1a) and (4a) are unambiguous: the Subject couldn't perform an action. I have no general explanation for why *with a thud* suppresses the action sense of *hit* in (2). In (3a), any Direct Object specifying a sensation suppresses the action sense of *feel*, and conversely any nonsensation Direct Object suppresses the sensation sense of *feel* in favor of the action sense. Hence, to read (3b) as a sensation, we must imagine some ellipsed material such as '(the touch of) her ankle'. In the other examples, manner adverbs (*boldly, carefully, tactfully, energetically*) and instrumental adverbial (*with a hammer*) select the action sense. The conjunction with another action verb in (1c) suggests a sequential narrative of John's actions.

The concept of action is one of the most obscure ones in common use. Primarily, the questions center on the relation of the Subject to the action. As before, at least three distinguishable traits appear to occur together in typical actions: the Subject is energy-source, cause of, and in control of, the action. It is relatively easy, however, to split these traits and thereby to raise classificatory problems:

cause: The crash drew a large crowd.
           The rotting fish is attracting flies.

energy: He sneezed/tripped/stumbled/threw up.

>   *control*:   He floated down the river to elude the search party.
>   The diver rose forty feet at a time to avoid the bends.

I will not pursue the question of whether ACTION is anything more than
a family resemblance here: the matter is discussed in Cruse (1973), Fodor
(1974), Dillon (1974), and many other places.

Inchoatives are verbs that express a change in their Subjects. Some
of them are quite happy with most adverbials of degree ('extent'), some
are not:

>   I. The colors faded a little.
>   Her finger swelled slightly/considerably.
>   It grew a good bit/somewhat.
>
>   II. It stopped/started (?somewhat).
>   He fainted (?a little).
>   The plane landed (?slightly).
>
>   He lost/won the election (?somewhat).
>   He realized his mistake (?a little).
>   He reached the top (?considerably).

The verbs of II have two further properties that distinguish them from
those of I: when progressive, the reading is 'has not yet *V*ed' (or 'is about
to *V*'), and they will take *in* + *(time interval)* adverbials instead of the
for + *(time interval)* adverbials that group I verbs take. Actually, most of
the group I verbs can also take *in* + *time interval* but then are reinterpreted
as group II:

>   The colors faded in two weeks. (= 'lost their original vividness')
>   It grew in two weeks. (= 'grew up' or 'grew to its present state')

or, in some cases, as 'start to *V*', which is again a group II sense:

>   Her finger swelled in five minutes.

(We are ignoring the 'within' sense of *in*.) Group II verbs have been called
Achievement verbs by Zeno Vendler (1967), Transitional Event verbs
(Quirk et al., 1972), absolute-process verbs (Chafe, 1970), and (one type
of) completive verbs (Dillon, 1973). Group I verbs may be called degree-
inchoatives (Chafe, 1970, calls them relative-process).

In terms of general intuitions, group I verbs express changes that have
no intrinsic end-point (to imagine them as of group II, we may imagine an
end-point given in context); hence, the change could "keep going on" indefinitely. The changes expressed by verbs of group II reach an end-point;
hence they cannot be said to have happened until the end-point is reached,
and duration becomes how long it takes to get to the end-point. One can

distinguish two subgroups in II, one where the transition is "sharp" (*lose the election, faint*), others where it is not (*stop,* [*a plane*] *land*). This latter group will take the modifiers *completely, fully, totally,* which give the effect of redundancy with *faint,* etc.:

> He didn't completely stop at the stop sign.
> Keep your seat belts fastened until the plane has completely landed.
> ?He completely fainted.
> ?He lost the election totally.

This last propery, however, is not so much a matter of the verb itself as a property of the whole sentence, or of the particular kind of action involved:

> He totally lost control.
> ?The leaf completely landed on the dog's head.

One could argue that in *lose control, control* is a MASS noun and *totally* really means 'lost total control', but this does not explain why (*a plane*) *land* can take *completely* but (*a leaf*) *land* cannot. Further, if *faint* is 'lose consciousness . . . ' , why won't it take *completely* (*consciousness* being a MASS noun)—or will it after all?

This second subclass of II shades into an intermediate group where the change toward an end-state is viewed as gradual enough (i.e., not a sharp transition) that *somewhat, slightly,* and *for + time interval* are ok with them (like degree-inchoatives) as well as *completely* and *in + time interval* (like Achievements):

> The wine ages $\left\{ \begin{array}{l} \text{for six months} \\ \text{somewhat} \end{array} \right\}$ before being bottled.
>
> The wine ages $\left\{ \begin{array}{l} \text{in six months} \\ \text{completely} \end{array} \right\}$ in the cask.

Other verbs with this amphibious property are *recover, wake up,* and *separate.* Predictably, the progressive can be taken either way, either as 'in process of' (as with degree-inchoatives) or as 'has not yet' (as with Achievements). Perhaps most Achievements are susceptible to "weakening" in the direction of degree-inchoatives. The picture that emerges is a continuum with some verbs marked as "sharp" Achievements on one end (*reach, faint*) and some interminable degree-inchoatives on the other end (*fade, grow*) with various "gradual" Achievements spread out in between.

2.4

Knowledge of the World

As should be already apparent, there are countless components one could abstract that play minor roles in selecting senses and have no other conse-

quences to speak of in the language. For example, there are several senses of *blind*, one of which is selected in *blind₁ child*, another in *blind₂ alley*. This latter sense can perhaps appear with other nouns like *corridor, tunnel, street*, and one could abstract a component PASSAGEWAY to express the selectional restriction of *blind₂*. In regard to this, and a number of other, more general, features, it seems silly to claim that the words *corridor, tunnel*, and *street* (and *burrow* . . .) all have the component PASSAGEWAY coded as part of their senses: all that is necessary is that they be regarded as passageways for the time being. Our eyebrows may rise, and we may begin to search for another sense, or a plausible extension of sense, purely on assumptions we hold about probable referents of terms. Consider the following curiosities:

> He stabbed it with his toothbrush.
> He broke the dog.
> He brushed the crumbs off the table with his car.

With *stab with X* there is a selectional restriction ⟨X POINTED OBJECT⟩ —if we assume that the probable referent is not pointed, we may extend the sense of *stab* to that of *stab at* ('jab at'), rather than imagine a pointed toothbrush. Similarly, *break X* has the selectional feature ⟨X RIGID⟩ for one sense. Given the usual assumptions about dogs, we might consider the 'tame' sense of *break* rather than imagine a rigid dog (context will make a great deal of difference, obviously—had there been talk establishing the dog as a stone one, there would be no hesitation here). The last example is similar—notice how it changes if *the boy* is substituted for *he*. It is also absurd to suppose that one associates CAN BE USED TO BRUSH with every object that could appear with *brush*. The term 'pragmatic considerations' is sometimes used to refer to the reasons we might balk at or reinterpret the sentences cited here.

2.5

M e t a p h o r
(a s R e c o n t e x t u a l i z a t i o n)

It has long been held that metaphor involves a novel or creative act of mind in user and hearer. We will view it as the creation, for the nonce, of adjusted sense for certain words. It will be useful to narrow the notion of adjustment to exclude cases like *by the Cosmic Construction Company*, where an extra component (LOCATION) is added to a word, by saying that the adjustment must include cancellation of some definitional component of the usual sense. Thus *Fort* in the following should probably be adjusted by cancelling the MILITARY STRONG POINT components in favor of the associated ones ENCLOSED PLACE and SUBJECT TO ASSAULT (so to speak):

> but yet could never win
> The Fort, that Ladies hold in soueraigne dread.

The criterion of cancellation will class *rose* below as a symbol or analogy rather than a metaphor, since the words retain their literal senses (*thy light*, however, is a metaphor). Othello is addressing the sleeping Desdemona:

(1)   but once put out thy light,
       Thou cunning'st pattern of excelling nature,
       I know not where is that Promethean heat
       That can thy light relume. When I have pluck'd the rose
       I cannot give it vital growth again.
       It needs must wither. I'll smell it on the tree. [*kisses her*]
                                        —*Othello,* V.ii. 10–15

Othello establishes a referential link between *the rose* and Desdemona, and the lines do associate rose-properties (beauty, fragility) with her, but no adjustment is necessary in the sense of *rose*.

   Obviously there is no need to construct an adjusted sense for a word if one knows another existing one that is adequate. As noted in the previous chapter, dictionaries frequently do list extended senses, many of which might be viewed as classifications of common metaphorical uses. Obviously, too, if one is unaware of a usable extended sense, he will have to construct one—as we become more familiar with literature and traditional metaphors, we can retrieve more from memory and engage in less construction of new adjusted senses. One might consider imposing a criterion for metaphor that no usage is metaphorical if the needed sense is listed in the dictionary. This would impose less uniformity than at first appears, however, because dictionaries differ in the amount of space and attention they devote to listing usual extended senses, and it would be rather artificial in regard to the individual reader's and writer's experience. We would also be claiming that hackneyed or well-worn metaphors are not metaphors—*the flames of passion* (*AHD: flame* 3. 'a violent or intense passion: a burning emotion'), *winter of our discontent* (*AHD: winter* 3. 'any period of time characterized by coldness, misery, barrenness, or death'). (Notice that this last is really a collection of metaphoric extensions, not all of which might be relevant in a given context.) If we give up the requirement of novelty, we then admit *fly* in

   The Sarazin . . . to him flew

as a metaphor, albeit a very moribund one, and similarly *arm of a chair* and *leg of the table*, but I do not see how to restrict the definition of metaphor to exclude these cases without making it wholly relative to the impression of the reader.

There must be some sort of incompatibility between the usual senses of the word and the context to trigger the search for a suitably adjusted sense. The incompatibility may range from anomaly:

(2)   Shame is a shawl of pink
(3)   poisoned hours had bound me up/From mine own knowledge

to factual improbability:

(4)   drink delicious poison from thy eye
(5)   I was/A morsel for a monarch

to lack of literal referent in the imagined scene:

(6)   [*Cleopatra speaking, Antony having gone to Rome*]
                                        He's speaking now,
           Or murmuring, "Where's my serpent of old Nile?"
           For so he calls me. Now I feed myself
           With most delicious poison.
                              —*Antony and Cleopatra*, I.v.24–27

to incongruity in context:

(7)   [*Othello's final speech*—"in speaking of me you must speak"]
                                        of one whose hand
           Like the base Judean, threw a pearl away
           Richer than all his tribe.
                              —*Othello*, V.ii.346–48

Not all incompatibilities point to metaphor, however. Contradictions, in particular, are often paradoxes that suggest a reality transcending human categories:

           And having lost her breath, she spoke, and panted,
           That she did make defect perfection
           And, breathless, power breathe forth.
                              —*Antony and Cleopatra*, II.ii.231–33

                but she makes hungry
           Where most she satisfies.
                              —*Antony and Cleopatra*, II.ii.238–39

Marvell's *green thought* probably belongs here ("The Garden," l. 48). The question must be not "Does this passage contain a metaphor?" but "Is this passage susceptible of metaphoric interpretation (i.e., by adjusting the sense of some word or words in it)?"

Having noted something amiss, and suspecting metaphor, <u>the reader
must decide which words to adjust</u>. In the case of the missing or unlikely
referent, the obvious adjustment would be in the problematic noun phrase
(*delicious poison, pearl, thy light*). In these cases, the adjustment will be
governed by what appears to be the referent in context: *pearl*, in a set of
statements concerning Othello's relation to Desdemona, need only have its
SPHERICAL, HARD, LUSTROUS, etc. components cancelled in favor
of the associated components PRECIOUS, BEAUTIFUL (*WNC: pearl* 2.
'one that is very choice or precious') to be able to refer to her. Here, as with
all metaphor, other associated properties of pearls (e.g., WHITE) may also
remain and be ascribed to Desdemona if not incompatible or irrelevant (in
the reader's judgment). *Throw away* will also have to be adjusted but will
retain the component AS VALUELESS in the adjusted sense. In (5) *morsel*
seems the likely term for adjustment. The example occurs a few lines after
(6) in Cleopatra's musing on her charms:

> Broad-fronted Caesar,
> When thou wast here above the ground, I was
> A morsel for a monarch; and great Pompey
> Would stand and make his eyes grow in my brow.
> —*Antony and Cleopatra*, I.v.29–32

The context suggests suppressing the SMALL BIT OF FOOD components
in favor of the associated DELICACY component (*WNC: morsel* 3b.
'something delectable and pleasing'). An element of sensual enjoyment is,
of course, conveyed by DELICACY. Notice how Antony's later, angry
simile blocks off this possibility:

> I found you as a morsel cold upon
> Dead Caesar's trencher; nay, you were a fragment
> Of Cneius Pompey's.
> —*Antony and Cleopatra*, III.xiii.116–18

It is not always obvious which term should be adjusted. In (2), which
is the first line of a poem by Emily Dickinson, one is uncertain whether to
adjust the sense of *shame* by adding something like PHYSICAL MANI-
FESTATION OF . . . , or of *shawl* by cancelling the GARMENT component while retaining the PROTECTIVE and other components. Actually,
adding a component to *shame* does not qualify as a metaphor under our
definition unless the added component is felt to conflict with an existing
definitional one, forcing its cancellation. This line is close to what is sometimes called mutual metaphor: <u>each term is adjusted by its association with
the other.</u>

These fairly simple examples are offered to show how context will shape our adjustment of meanings. The next and final example is a bit more complicated, for to process it we must proceed on two levels and draw on a bit of factual knowledge:

> Everything that man esteems
> Endures a moment or a day.
> Love's pleasure drives his love away,
> The painter's brush consumes his dreams;
> The herald's cry, the soldier's tread
> Exhaust his glory and his might:
> Whatever flames upon the night
> Man's own resinous heart has fed.
> > —W. B. Yeats, "Two Songs from a Play"

Heart in the last line is a kind of double metaphor. To get the metaphorical sense of *resinous, heart* must be the source of the metaphorical flames— wood—with respect to which *resinous* ascribes the property of resinous wood—volatility of a certain sort. The volatile heart feeds *whatever flames* —the 'passion' extension is easy—and the context narrows the range of the usual extended senses of *heart* to 'desire', allowing *whatever flames* to generalize all of the passions mentioned (love, vision of beauty, glory, etc.), so that we come out with something like 'human desire is the source of all human passions.' The metaphors contribute certain associated components: desire is ingrained, volatile, inward, and the vital core of man self-consumed in the blaze. There is an old saying that the advantage of metaphor is that it gives you two ideas for one—actually, it gives you a whole bunch, but not all.

The ability to decontextualize word senses and to code the range of contexts in which the sense may operate is essential for human language, since the learner thereby becomes able to recombine words into new sentences without any doubt that the new sentences will be well-formed if the words satisfy the selectional requirements of other words. The next chapter will describe the techniques of decontextualization applied to parts of words. These techniques are useful, and probably are applied by learners to various degrees, but there is a crucial limitation to the freedom to form new words that distinguishes decontextualization at the word level from that at the phrase and sentence level.

READINGS FOR CHAPTER II

Selectional components are well discussed in Chafe (1970) and Gruber (1967) and briefly touched in most introductions to transformational grammar, among which Langendoen (1969) is the most adequate. All of these accounts give rise to the view that selectional components are part of the senses of the words that match them—the incorrectness of this view is argued in Fillmore (1971a) and Lakoff (1971b).

A classic work on anomaly and metaphor is Weinreich (1966), where the possibility of adjusting a selectional clash in either direction is entertained (p. 465, n. 92).

Fillmore (1974) emphasizes that constructing a figuratively extended reading draws on factual knowledge and beliefs. So also Black (1962) and Beardsley (1962). For some recent discussions see *Poetics* 14/15 (Vol. IV, no. 2/3, 1975).

Although generalizations about restrictions of partitive expressions are hard to come by in English, major ones are possible in various oriental languages with "classifiers"—the basis of the restrictions is usually visual form. See Adams and Conklin (1974). Friedrich (1972) is an interesting survey of classifiers in a wide variety of languages.

Loewenberg (1975) argues convincingly that metaphor cannot be defined solely in terms of semantic anomaly. The 'morsel for a monarch' example is hers.

Thomas (1968) treats metaphor purely in terms of anomaly and views the process of sense-adjustment rather rigidly. The 'Shame is a shawl of pink' example is his.

EXERCISES AND PROBLEMS

1. Which are anomalous, which contradictory, or contradictions?
   (a) The dog elapsed. anomalous
   (b) My uncle is pregnant. cont.
   (c) John invented a four-legged tripod. cont.
   (d) John's speech upset the square root of 2. anom.
   (e) The little pine tree grew wise in the ways of the forest. anomalous
   (f) He broke the water into pieces. cont.
   (g) My sister is an only child. cont.

2. What is the selectional restriction on *present* (= 'current')? contingent?

3. Classify the following verbs according to the type of change expressed:
   deteriorate, freeze, increase, forget, remember
   I   II   I

4. Quirk et al. (1972) report that
   Her son is grown.   action of growing is finished
   is dubious in British English, where *grown up* is preferred. What sort of distinction does the British speaker make?

5. Does the use of *die* in the following require setting up a sense distinct from 'come to be dead/cease to be alive'?   dying is here a slow process
   We die a little every day. —

6. What class of verbs can take a Benefactive such as *for Mary* (= 'for her benefit' or 'on her behalf')? actions

7. Is the paraphrase of *bachelor* as 'one who has never been married' correct?

8. Are the following phrases susceptible of metaphoric interpretation? *vague.*
   cloud of fragrance/invisible cloud/cloud of suspicion

   And these sentences:
   After a cigarette, he called her back.
   It's about three hours to Chicago.

9. *AHD* gives two senses for *loaf*, the second of which is: *OK*
   2. any shaped mass of food: *veal loaf.*
   This seems a little too general—a chopped-chicken-liver loaf? What components would you add to represent the restrictions on your use of it?

10. The following oddities probably do not reflect selectional restrictions, but some general restriction does seem to be involved in at least the first set. Try to work out an informal statement of the restriction(s).

   (a) 1. He was so rich he snored.
       2. He was too drunk to get chicken pox.
       3. He was not intelligent enough to paint his bathroom purple. *vague!*

   (b) 1. He hammered the metal triangular/cylindrical/square.
       2. He hammered the metal beautiful/safe/dangerous.
       3. He hammered the rod bent/crooked.

11. Write out definitions, if you know them, for the following terms and analyze them into form/function: *awl, center-punch, nail-set, reamer, countersink, tap* (only the tool senses). *relation between physical characteristics and functions*

12. What explanation can you offer for the fact that one might say
        I am dying. *→ can be a long process*
   but not
        I am fainting. (Rather: I am going to faint.)
              too sharp or sudden a process to be used as a progressive form.

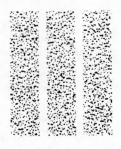

The Structure
of Words

Just as the meanings of sentences may be viewed as compositions of the meanings of words, so the meanings of many words can be viewed as compositions of the meanings of parts of words. There is a crucial difference, however: speakers can form countless combinations of words and expect to be understood, but they cannot form words with this freedom and expect to be understood. One can usually "compute" the readings of sentences and phrases in terms of the senses of the component words previously decontextualized, but one cannot always predict from the structure of a word its precise sense (or senses), and there are many words that should be well-formed that don't exist. Nonetheless, the structure may provide clues to the senses of words, and certain words cannot on semantic grounds have certain senses (i.e., would be "anomalous").

There are numerous thorny formal and theoretical questions (which are beyond the scope of this book) about how to represent these semi-generalizations (see the Readings), and it is an open question whether and to what extent speakers actually form and use them. A natural way to approach these matters is once again from the imaginary point of view of imaginary learners trying to guess the meanings of words they do not know and to work out the semantic conditions on word formation.

3.1

The Transparency of Words

The fundamental assumption is that learners will try to apply the techniques of decontextualization useful in learning meanings of whole words to parts of words. To review the first of these, consider the process of decontextualizing a sense for *will* from the following sentences:

> He will leave town next Tuesday.
> The mud will harden during the night.
> He will stop growing in another year.

It is easy to associate with *will* an element of prediction, which, moreover, appears to be totally unrestricted by any selectional considerations (versus *must₂* in Section 3.2). The same techniques seem attractive for *re-* in the following sentences:

> Shortly after closing it, they had to reopen the safe.
> Because it was so close, they recounted the votes.
> It melted when brought inside but refroze when put back out.

Here it would be elementary to postulate that some AGAIN component is the sense contributed to the sentence by *re-* (there are selectional restrictions to be discussed shortly). When we come to *reinterpret* and *rewrite*, however, a problem arises in that the sense of these words is not perfectly paraphrased as 'interpret again', 'write again', because there appears to be an associated component TO IMPROVE with *rewrite* and a component DIFFERENTLY with *reinterpret*. These components show up with other formations also: *reconsider, retrain, rearrange*. Should the learners postulate one sense of *re-*, or two, or three? Perhaps the IMPROVE and DIFFERENTLY components should not be coded as part of the sense or senses of *re-*. We could account for their appearance with certain words by certain schemes of inference: doing something over might be done to improve the result or at least to change the result by doing it differently. *Recount*, for instance, is vague about whether one should do it differently. Similarly, one might *rewrite* something to make it harder to comprehend (as linguists sometimes do, or composition teachers). In any case, while the IMPROVE or DIFFERENTLY components might come to be associated with particular *re* + *Verb* forms (or be definitional, in the cases of *rearrange* and *reinterpret*), it is perhaps overloading *re-* itself to say that they are part of its sense or senses. Further, it would appear to predict too many senses for *re-* verbs: *rearrange*, for example, would be ambiguous over senses 'ARRANGE AGAIN', 'ARRANGE AGAIN DIFFERENTLY', and 'AR-RANGE AGAIN to IMPROVE', and this seems silly. Taking the "one sense" solution has one cost attached: the senses of the resulting verbs will be slightly unpredictable.

The problem of idiosyncrasy of combined meanings arises for words far more pointedly than for phrases and sentences, because speakers tend to treat words as the basic units of meaning. Using a word in a slightly un-usual way is quite normal, but using whole phrases in slightly extended ways is very strange (though it may be the source of idioms). Looked at the other way, speakers expect that the meaning of phrases and sentences can be made out by certain general rules from the senses of the individual words, and they honor that assumption in their usage, but they do not equally as-sume that the meanings of words can be predicted from their "parts."

To see the effect of specialization and shifting of a basically predicta-ble sense, consider the word *telescopic*, which receives five senses in the *AHD*:

> *1.* Of or pertaining to a telescope.
> *2.* Seen through or obtained by means of a telescope.
> *3.* Visible only by means of a telescope.
> *4.* Able to discern distant objects; farseeing.
> *5.* Extensible or compressible by or as if by the successive sliding of over-lapping concentric tubular sections.

Looking up *-ic*, one finds 'of, pertaining to, or characteristic of', so that of these senses (1) is wholly predictable, and so are (4) and (5), conceding that there is no way we could expect *-ic* to predict which particular charac-teristic of telescopes would be picked out. Senses (2) and (3) are irregular in terms of the general definition of *-ic*, though they turn up in *microscopic*. Postulating two new senses of *-ic* would enable us to generalize these senses of these words, but probably not very many others, so the authorities do not bother to list these as established senses of *-ic*.

Our hypothetical learners have yet to deal with the tougher *re-* words. They might group the following as potentially involving another, new, sense of *re-*:

re-call	reenter (the atmosphere)
return	re-dress (put clothes back on)
refund	repossess

and might construct a vague sense for *re₂-*: BACK, but it must be a little vague, since these words do not mean precisely '*V* back'—rather there is some notion of something going back to where it was before. I suspect that this vagueness is functional, if we want to capture inferential strategies that people may use.

Our learners have finally to deal with a residue class, none of which is hyphenated in print (but hyphenation is not too reliable as a clue to plausible segmentations, as the previous set showed):

receive	resist	recede
reduce	remit	recur
refine	refer	respond

These are notorious cases where some knowledge of Latin makes many of the words less opaque (i.e., a bit more guessable), though one is very hard-pressed to define a sense or senses for *re-* that will work for them all. It is hard to guess, on the face of it, what our learners will do here. There is some reason, however, to believe that some speakers do something.

What speakers actually code for prefixes and suffixes is an empirical question, and there should be some ways of inferring it from what people do with words. Several approaches have been suggested by various writers. Any "productive" (i.e., novel) formation by speakers indicates they have decontextualized the prefix: "I told him to rebutter the toast." Similarly, children who coin terms like *sweeper* (for broom) and *brusher* (for brush) show that they have decontextualized the *-er* suffix with the sense 'what one uses to *V*'. Closely related is the evidence one can get from "mistakes": many people use *nauseous* with the sense "having nausea" (though 88 percent of the *AHD*'s usage panel oppose this usage). The "mistake" is a reasonable one, however, since *N* + *ous* almost always means 'having *N*'. This word is the word-level analogue of a semi-idiom (like *blade of grass*): the meaning of *nauseous* is not what its parts would predict. The only other word where *-ous* combines with a verb yielding the sense 'tends to *V*' is *poisonous*. Here we could postulate a sense of *-ous* that it has when it combines with two verbs, but plainly many speakers prefer to ignore this odd sense and treat *nauseous* as regular. A third way of gathering clues is to ask people to paraphrase unfamiliar words like *deobnoxify, microphonic, subsert*, or *reswap*, and a fourth way is the "forced-choice" variant of the third, where, for example, speakers would be asked to choose as a paraphrase for *subsert* either (a), (b), or (c):

(a) upset something by pushing from below
(b) push something under something
(c) sink to the bottom of

One such questionnaire appears in the exercises for this chapter. In general, the answers are not randomly distributed, indicating that some kind of common "knowledge" is being drawn on. Some work of this nature has been done with compound nouns and will be discussed below.

The overall picture that our hypothetical learners get of the predictability of word senses is of a transparency gradient or cline. Some senses are exactly what decontextualization and recombination(!) would predict, others are less so but not far off, others only murkily like the prediction, and a few wrong (*nauseous*). The number of cases a putative sense of an affix would predict ranges from many (*re₁-*) to few (lesser senses of *-ic, -ous*), and it is plausible on the face of it that learners might differ considerably in the degree to which they actually decontextualize senses for affixes, as opposed to coding the meanings of words as unsystematized wholes, and further, that the degree to which they do this might correlate with verbal aptitude. This is speculation worth some investigation.

3.2

Selectional Rules

In the decontextualization described so far, the learners have only performed half of the procedure normal for words in phrases and sentences—they have not yet attempted to specify the selectional restrictions between affix (prefix or suffix) and stem. Again to review the procedure at the sentence level, some of the sentences below are ambiguous over two readings of *must,* others have only one sense:

> He must run very fast.
> Those stockings must run very readily.

> He must pay his bills promptly.
> He must resemble his father.

> He must float down the river at night.
> The wood must float down the river at night.

The *must₁* of inference is always possible—there are no restrictions—but the *must₂* of obligation is possible only where obligation itself makes sense, namely with verbs viewed as CONTROLLABLE by a human Subject. Thus we can state the restriction for *must₂* in general selectional components (in angular brackets) as:

> X *must₂* V: [X OBLIGATED to V] $\langle V$ CONTROLLABLE BY X &
> X HUMAN$\rangle$

Now consider *re₁-*. It cannot attach to just any verb: the verb must be modifiable by *again*. Hence, each of the following pairs is equally bad, ignoring *again* as a sentence modifier (i.e., ?"It has again come to be the case that . . . "):

*The rock has weighed twenty grams again.
*The rock has reweighed twenty grams.

*The rock has cost twenty dollars a ton again.
*The rock has recost twenty dollars a ton.

There are sentences, however, where *again* modifies the verb happily enough but *re* + *Verb* is surprisingly odd:

He has forgotten his English again.
?He has reforgotten his English.

He has fainted again.
?He has refainted.

The ball has rolled into the pocket again.
?The ball has rerolled into the pocket.

Apparently it is necessary, but not sufficient, for the verb to be of the right selectional class to predict the existence of a word *re* + *Verb*. Verbs like *refaint* are sometimes called 'possible words' that don't happen to exist. The contrast with selectional restrictions between words is very sharp: one cannot say that there are possible but nonexisting sentences.

Consider two further parallel cases. Many adjectives can be used as verbs with the meaning 'come to be more *ADJ*' (i.e., as Type I degree-inchoatives). Some require a suffix such as *-en* (*darken, widen, harden*) or *-ify* (*solidify*), others go without a suffix (*calm, cool*). An apparently necessary condition is that the adjective have a sense which is usually called **gradable**: one can speak of being 'more *ADJ*'. Thus it is more or less predictable that there is no verb *false* or *falsify* meaning 'become more false' or *pregnantify* 'become more pregnant'. (As a causative, however, *falsify* is ok—apparently the restriction applies only, or primarily, for the inchoative meaning.) Note that this principle predicts that the inchoative sense of *deaden* must have to do with a sense of *dead* other than the nongradable 'has ceased to live'. Here the selectional restriction (which can be regarded as introduced by MORE and hence redundant for *-en*)

X-en: [COME TO BE MORE *X*] ⟨*X* GRADABLE⟩

does operate to select a sense of *dead* compatible with it (i.e., become 'numb, diminished in intensity, etc.'). There are, however, many gradable adjectives that have no inchoative verbs paired with them (e.g., *wet, sorry, able*). Hence gradability is necessary but not sufficient to predict the existence of the inchoative verb formed from the adjective.

The last example concerns the formation of resultative nouns from verbs. Many nouns, formed from verbs with a variety of suffixes or no suffix, have a sense 'that which has come to be as a result of *V*ing':

    growth
    interpretation/decomposition
    seepage/wreckage
    painting/learning/clipping
    arrangement/development
    catch/toast/cut/burn/rise/break/decay

Apparently some sort of change must be going on [* a simmering/*a seep-(age)], and this selectional restriction selects one sense of *turn$_v$* in

    He made a sharp turn.

by blocking the 'rotate' sense, among others, but there seems no way to predict *break* and *seepage* but exclude **shatter, *gush(age, ing)*. In sum, the semantic constraints can mark certain formations as anomalous and select certain senses of verbs, but they do not guarantee the existence of words that are compatibly formed.

3.3

Compound Nouns

Suppose our imaginary learners have acquired a goodly list of deverbal nouns (*growth, mower, damage*) and further that they encounter such constructions as those italicized:

    I've got to cut the grass. Where is the *lawn mower*?
    She picked up the soup can in her left claw and shoved it into the *can
        opener*.
    These clippers are only good for grass. I want *hedge clippers*.

It would be possible for them without much difficulty to infer that the sense of each compound is 'what one uses to *VN*' and to abstract this pattern of interpretation. Encountering

    wood cutter
    house painter
    truck driver

which would in context usually refer to animate entities, they could infer a second pattern 'one who *VsN*'. Then when they came across such terms as

    pea classer
    dog chaser

they could with some confidence postulate as senses 'one who or that which classes peas, chases dogs'.

Slightly different is a group of sets where the first noun is understood to specify the second, deverbal noun. The first of these sets

food poisoning	have as a general paraphrase	'poisoning caused by food'
sun burn		'burn caused by sun'
storm damage		'damage caused by storm'

$$N_2 \text{ caused by } N_1$$

Other sets in this group are:

steam cleaning	N_2 done with N_1
gun fight	
sliderule calculation	

heart failure	N_2 of N_1
population growth	
earthquake	
card playing	
blood test	
mail delivery	

home cooking	N_2 at/on/in N_1
boat ride	
room service	

For all of these, the sense of the compound can be at least roughly paraphrased as a sentence in which the verb is the one underlying the second (deverbal) noun and the first plays some role in relation to it. As a construction type—Noun + deverbal Noun—it is indeterminate with respect to the exact role played by the first noun, but the learner is not at an utter loss in guessing the range of alternatives. Where two alternatives are plausible, the compound is ambiguous: *Food poisoning is bad.*

There is a parallel set of compounds where the deverbal element is first, the related noun second, and again roughly the same range of possible roles appears:

retaining wall	N_2 that Vs (where V = verb underlying N_1)
scrub woman	
demolition squad	

washing machine	N_2 that one uses to V
drinking cup	
grindstone	
playing card	

asking price	N_2 that is Ved
smelling salts	
push button	

swimming pool N_2 where one Vs
playground
storage battery

A third major set of compound nouns that our learners will encounter differs from the foregoing in that the verbal element is missing. There are two nouns, and the interpretation of the compound depends on the relation that is understood to obtain between them. The relations again form sets:

ash tray	coffee cream	N put on/in N
brief case	eye wash	(either order)
flower box	shoe polish	
coat rack	spaghetti sauce	

candle light	water pistol	N gives/produces N
battle fatigue	Coke machine	
blood stain		
fever blister		

	oil well	N_1 taken/obtained from N_2
	coal mine	
	silk worm	
	honey bee	
	sugar beet	

	apple sauce	N_2 made from N_1
	grape wine	
	peanut butter	

alcohol lamp		N_2 powered by N_1
air rifle		
windmill		

	bug spray	N_2 to keep N_1 away
	gas mask	
	heat shield	
	mosquito net	

	life boat	N_2 to retain/keep/preserve N_1
	cash box	
	dog leash	
	safety belt	

	mailman	N_2 carries/conveys N_1
	milk truck	
	oil pipe	

| | dragonfly | N_2 resembles N_1 |
| | kettledrum | |

Perhaps the learners will not be sure whether to class certain compounds as "give" or "take" compounds—the semantic shading is delicate, having to do with whether the source is understood to 'emit' the substance or to 'yield' it—but again, they can at least approximate the senses of these compounds in terms of these basic (abstracted) relations. They can, but do they?

There are a number of reasons to believe that these patterns are in fact abstracted by learners. Gleitman and Gleitman (1971) note that when asked what they would call a dog that brings the mail, younger children will reply 'a dog mailman', but adults will reply a 'maildog', indicating that they have analyzed (presumably reanalyzed) *mailman* in terms of the next to last pattern cited. In general, if you make up strange compounds and ask people to paraphrase them, they will often give one or more paraphrases from the basic patterns (usually only the more probable ones: a *turkey tree* is unlikely to be paraphrased as 'a tree one takes turkeys from').

Gleitman and Gleitman show, however, that not all of these patterns may be equally functioning for speakers. They asked informants to paraphrase a set of double compounds that included such exotic items as:

(1)   house-bird wash
        house-kill bird

(2)   wash bird-house
        bird kill-house

(3)   foot bird-house
        bird boot-house

Type (3) is derived by the third type of compounding (i.e., Noun + Noun) applied twice; hence it yields such paraphrases as:

      foot bird-house: 'a bird-house for feet'
                          'a ground apartment for birds'
      bird boot-house: 'a house where boots for birds are kept'

Although there are some errors and misinterpretations, the type (3) compounds are quite a bit more reliably paraphrased than type (1) and (2), taken as a group, and (2) is less reliably paraphrased than (1). Types (1) and (2) involve at least one application of the deverbal Noun derivations (here only with zero suffix), so that for (1) we should get

      house-bird wash: 'something you use to wash house-birds'
                          'an event when you wash all the house-birds'
                          'the weekly wash that the house-birds do'
      house-kill bird: 'a bird that kills in houses'
                          'a bird that kills houses'

and for (2)

wash bird-house: 'a bird-house for washing—where one washes'
bird kill-house: 'a place where one kills birds'

Admittedly, it is hard to imagine why one would ever want to use some of
these compounds, given our assumptions about birds and their behavior,
but the point is that speakers "know" what these compounds would have
to mean if they came across them. This "knowledge" is not evenly distributed over the three types, however, and the results suggest that deverbal
patterns are less established in the minds of speakers than the Noun + Noun
pattern (3) and further that the Noun + deverbal Noun pattern (*food poisoning*) is more established than the deverbal Noun + Noun (*retaining wall*)
type. (This inference would stand on firmer ground if the deverbal types
with affixes could be investigated.) The Gleitmans noted a very sharp difference between their graduate-student informants and those with less education, suggesting that the ability to draw on these patterns was far more
developed in the graduate students. The sixty-four-dollar psycholinguistic
question is: what do 'developed' and 'established in the mind' mean? That,
and the whole set of questions having to do with how and to what degree
speakers actually make the generalizations that are possible, are topics
needing much more investigation.

READINGS FOR CHAPTER III

General handbooks on word formation in English are Marchand (1969), Adams
(1973), and the Appendix of Quirk et al. (1972). Lees (1970) is most important
for nominal derivations.
    Models of derivational regularity within the paradigm of generative gram-
mar are set forth in Gruber (1967), Lakoff (1970), Chomsky (1971b), Jackendoff
(1975), and in part in Levi (1974).
    Leech (1974, Chapter 10) is an interesting account of limited regularity.

EXERCISES AND PROBLEMS

1. Both members of each of the following pairs can be paraphrased by one of
   the patterns described in the chapter. For each pair, give the first compound
   used to exemplify the pattern in the text. Example:

                     opium poppy   type: oil well
                     stone quarry

   (a) nose drops   *coffee cream*   (c) insane asylum   *life boat*
       steak sauce   rabbit hutch

   (b) noise filter   *bug spray*   (d) hydrogen bomb *alcohol lamp*
       flu vaccine   oil stove

(e) cold sore   (h) sword play
    ink blot   tongue lashing
(f) nose bleed $N_L \, of \, N_1$ (i) baking powder   washing machine
    tooth decay   modeling clay
(g) fault-finding $N_2 \, of \, N_1$ (j) ironing board
    wage freeze   parking lot

2. What semantic restrictions are there on the verbs that can yield adjectives according to the patterns:

           (a) self-*V*ing   (b) *V*able
        must: Action   〈STATIVE〉

3. Make up five sentences, each one of which uses *telescopic* in one of the five different senses cited from the *AHD*.

4. You may be interested in comparing your answers to the following "questionnaire" with those of some English professors (given in the Answers):

abducive   a. informing   *egredient*   that which is
              b. distracting   a. smoothed
              c. conserving   b. held
                                                    c. vaporized
supponent   a. fundamental
              b. excessive   *arrective*   a. raising
              c. softening   b. retarding
                                                    c. impairing
erigible   capable of being
              a. twisted   *degressive*   a. going down
              b. raised   b. coming up
              c. bent   c. turning around

(This questionnaire is adapted from one discussed by Lise Menn and Ronnie Wilbur in an LSA paper in Amherst, Mass., Summer, 1974.)

5. How could one infer the meaning of *ydrad* in the lines from *The Faerie Queen* cited on p. 28, given that *y*- is an old marker of past participle?

IV

Modification

Several references were made in the preceding chapter to rules for computing the readings of phrases and sentences from the senses of individual words. There is general agreement that such rules must exist, but their formalization is highly controversial, and the attempt to formulate them has led to greater awareness of the diversity and complexity of apparently simple phrasal relations. This chapter will survey some of the semantic differences underlying the relations of adjective to noun modified and duration adverbial to verb modified. The general definition of *modify* in traditional grammars—'to qualify or limit the meaning of'—suggests that one has simply to add the components of the adjective's or adverbial's sense to those of the noun or verb to get the reading for the phrase. So a noun refers to a set of individuals having certain properties, and the adjective would narrow the set to the subset having the property attributed by the adjective. Similarly, the duration adverbial would limit the time over which the relation predicated by the verb held. It will quickly appear, however, that the learner must learn to combine these components in a number of different ways.

Attributive Adjectives

This survey will be limited to noun phrases of the form *ADJ-Noun*. Roughly eight types of relations can be discriminated if "nouns used attributively" are included:

(1) beautiful wife
    stingy father-in-law

(2) blind dog
    red car

(3) large car
    small dog

(4) good car
    wrong house

(5) old friend
    late president

(6) joint undertaking
    lazy student

(7) suspected murderer
    fake revolver

(8) stone cistern
    woolen sweater

The first pair illustrate what Dwight Bolinger (1967) and other writers call nonrestrictive modification on the analogy to nonrestrictive relative clauses. Here one would suppose that *beautiful* does not narrow the possible range of referents of *wife*, since it presumably has only one member, but rather that it adds an attribute such as an appositive or nonrestrictive relative clause would:

wife, who is beautiful,
wife, and she is beautiful,

Said in a culture practicing polygamy, these phrases might be restrictive, though they need not be if all the relevant wives are beautiful, fathers-in-law stingy.

The set-theoretical notion of set intersection, which is plainly not relevant to nonrestrictive attribution, does seem to give an adequate account of the composed reading of the phrases in (2). The phrase *red car* picks out the possible referents of *car* that have the property of being red, or denotes the set of objects that are in the set of things that are red and also in the set of things that are cars. Similarly, *blind dog* denotes the objects that are dogs and that are also incapable of sight. The properties attributed by the adjective seem to involve target values on a physical or other continuum (*bald, straight, equilateral*) or discrete properties like *female* and *four-legged*. One can determine whether something is "*ADJ*" without determining what it is. Traditionally this type has been taken as the prototype of adjectival modification, but the property of being able to determine the denotation of the adjective independently of that of the noun is not shared by types (3)–(7).

The phrases in (3) cannot be interpreted in terms of set intersection. This is evident from the fact that *small dog* does not entail *small mammal*: if the denotation of *small dog* were in fact the intersection of the things that are small and the things that are dogs, then it would be in the set of dogs and hence in the set of mammals. The problem is obviously that there is no way to pick out on independent grounds the set of things that are small. Usually what is said is that adjectives of this type are covert comparatives with, e.g., the following general sense of *small*:

small *N*: SIZE of *N* LESS than AVERAGE SIZE of *N*s

though other norms might be understood in certain contexts: if a third-grade teacher is speaking to a pupil's parent when he says:

Henry is a tall boy.

something like 'taller than the typical boy of his age' or 'taller than the typical third-grader' or 'taller than the typical boy in the class' would be understood trather than simply 'taller than the typical boy'.

The parameters for physical properties do not exhaust the adjectives of this set. Others that come to mind are *expensive, stupid, difficult*. Many of these adjectives can float in and out of the class (this point is nicely discussed in Chafe, 1970: Chapter 11): 'If it costs over $1000, it's expensive no matter what it is'; 'If it will burn you, it's hot'; etc. It is worth noting, too, that when the adjective refers to a condition of (the referent of) the noun (*warm, cool, damp*), the Norm is understood to be 'than it usually is' or 'than one expected it to be' or 'than it was before'.

A curious fact about these adjectives when used as predicates

The painting is expensive.
An elephant is large.

is that they lose the sense of the norm for the class of *painting* and *elephant* and can spread to broader norms such as 'expensive for a wall decoration', 'for a home furnishing', 'for the work of an unknown artist', or 'for a land-going mammal', 'for an animal', etc. Chafe (1970: 194–96) suggests this is always a shift up one notch on the taxonomic hierarchy of the Subject noun, but perhaps this is only the strategy one would employ if there were no clues from context as to the relevant norm being applied.

Group (4) adjectives share the property of no independent denotation with those of group (3) but raise extra problems for us in picking out the property of the noun they operate on. Evidently there is no independently determinable class of things-that-are-good of which certain cars are a member. These adjectives evaluate (the referents of) nouns, but where the previous set of adjectives apply to a specific property or condition of the noun (*expensive*: ⟨COST⟩; *stupid*: ⟨INTELLIGENCE⟩), there are a number of properties that *good* might apply to. Jerrold Katz (1966) points out that where the noun involves some functional or instrumental components, these will be assumed to be the basis of the evaluation. Thus, *a good hammer* would probably praise the qualities of the hammer having to do with its use in pounding (weight, balance, trueness of striking face to handle, etc.) This line of thought suggests why *good grain of sand* strikes us as odd—though not hopeless, if we were given some context in which some function or use of grains of sand were in the air. Something like what Katz suggests does seem to be involved, since *good father* selects the nonbiological (i.e., the functionally defined) sense of *father*, but it is perhaps unnecessary to suppose that the parameter of evaluation is coded as such for each noun (which is Katz's proposal): one might simply state certain principles of evaluation that may be triggered by various components either in the definition of a word or associated with the word. This seems attractive when one considers terms like *dog* or *car*, where a number of criteria might be drawn on, depending on how one regarded the referent of the noun (what is the general duty, function, use, or purpose of a dog?). It is well known that for some things, the "official" and real purpose or function may be quite different: many people maintain that a good newspaper must have good comic pages (esthetic judgment). Several complexities are involved in judgments about *cars*: people differ in their view of the function of cars and the weight they give to different parts of the "function" (reliability, economy, comfort?, status?).

Certain hypotheses suggest themselves concerning the acquisition of evaluative adjectives. If the notion that children tend to reconceptualize things in terms of their purposes, uses, and functions (as adults conceive them) as they grow older is generally valid, the bases of their evaluations should change as more complex considerations become available to them. I notice a transition in my three-year-old daughter's use of *good*, which was at first primarily applied to animals and other children, meaning 'is friendly and does not threaten or do harm (to me)'. A new element was then added, however, 'obedient', in regard to the dog and herself. There are still elements to the adult judgment of *good dog* that escape her ('is decently housebroken', 'does not bark a lot', 'puts up with provocation', 'does not demand too much attention')—all of which may come under the general function of 'house pet', but which involve a very adult conception of behavior and decorum—not, of course, shared by all adults. It would be interesting to know how children of various ages answered "What is a good dog, knife, car, house?"

Note that with *right* and *wrong* the context is overwhelmingly important. The best that one can paraphrase out of context is 'in accordance with the relevant standard'—which is one of the reasons people can argue about what is right. Curiously enough, dictionaries seem to have overlooked the sense of *right* in such common usages as

That's not the right book. Bring me the other one.

where the "standard" is nothing more general than the speaker's intentions.

Types (5) and (6) probably need not be distinguished formally, but they are separated here for ease of reference. The modifiers of (5) are the temporal ones mentioned in the second chapter and modify some tensable entity in the sense of the word. *Old friend* is actually ambiguous over two readings, the intended one here ('one who has been my friend of old') and one of type (2) modification ('one that is my friend and that is old'). The use of temporal modifiers is not totally free, however: ?*my recent friend*. Note that there is a difference between *former President* and *late President* with respect to what is "past": both entail that the referent is no longer President but for different reasons. One places his Presidency in the past, the other, his existence. There is an interesting discussion and formalization of these constructions in John Anderson (1973).

Type (6) has in common with (5) the essentially adverbial nature of the modifier and is possible wherever there is a modifiable verb in the sense:

sloppy typist
lazy janitor
eager student

These are all ambiguous over two readings, one that is paraphrasable as 'one who types sloppily', 'one who maintains premises, etc., sloppily', 'one who studies eagerly', and one that is of type (2) modification: 'one who is sloppy and who is a typist'. The type (6) modification seems more probable as the noun is more transparently deverbal, the adjective less likely to refer to an unfluctuating personal trait. Linda Waugh (1976) notes that French places the adjective before the noun when it is "adverbial" (i.e., modifies some part of the sense of the noun), but following the noun when it attributes a property to the referent directly. Thus one gets contrasts like

vieil ami : friend of long standing
ami vieux : aged friend

furieux menteur : a furious liar (lies extravagantly, a lot)
menteur furieux : one who is a liar and who is angry

Type (7) also places conditions on the attribution of the properties to the referent, but not temporal conditions: they have to do with how well the actual referent satisfies the criteria of the noun. For all of the types so far considered, an *ADJ N* is still, or was, or will be, an *N*, but a *suspected murderer* is not necessarily a *murderer* but rather 'one who is suspected of murder' or essentially 'one who some think is a murderer'. The type includes the phrase *imitation gun* from the exercises of Chapter I as well as *imaginary friend* and perhaps the hedge-words discussed in Chapter I, most of which say that the referent of the phrase lacks some of the definitional characteristics of the *N*. Also in the group would be *possible answer, sure winner, likely candidate*. All of these "modalize" or limit the speaker's liability for attributing all of the properties associated with the noun to the referent.

I have included type (8) as an *ADJ-N* type on the strength of a very few forms (*wooden, woolen, silken, earthen*), since these are adjectives, but have separated them from type (2), though they are semantically like (2), because they lead to the very common use of nouns as attributes. *WNC* notes that certain nouns are used often enough as attributes to be so noted (*often attrib.*) but that almost any noun can be used attributively on occasion. In attributive use anything goes, from straight set intersection (*baby alligator*) through the compound types *copper pipe, hall carpet, garden vegetable* to the basic adjectival meaning 'of or pertaining to' (*freeway landscaping, city sewage plant*). These attributive formations may drift into compounds if one thinks that the entity so referred to is somehow a distinctly different thing rather than a special instance of the first thing:

hall cárpet vs. báthroom carpet
bathroom rúg

freeway lándscaping vs. freéway design (as in: 'I'm majoring in . . . ')
gas heáting vs. gás deregulation

(the heaviest stress falls on the Noun in a modifier-Noun sequence, but on the first Noun in a compound—but not always: see Valerie Adams, 1973: 110: *cottage cheése, midnight sún*).

As mentioned at the outset, the facts surveyed in this section are familiar to all working in linguistic semantics, and there are many models of semantic structure that represent some of them. I will summarize the observations by tabulating the types with paraphrases that attempt to record the logical properties discussed, though even the paraphrases are somewhat inexplicit:

(1) *beautiful wife*: one that is a wife and that is beautiful
(2) *red car*: one that is a car that is red
(3) *large car*: one that is a car with size greater than average size of cars
(4) *good car*: one that is a car that is good on some parameter(s)
(5) *old friend*: one that is of old a friend
(6) *joint undertaking*: one that is an action that is undertaken jointly
(7) *suspected murderer*: one that is suspected of being a murderer
(8) *woolen sweater*: one that is a sweater that is made of wool

Research on the acquisition of adjectives has centered on the acquisition of relative (type 3) adjectives. Imagine how odd it must seem to a child to hear a six-inch spoon referred to as a big spoon and a twelve-inch lamp referred to as a small lamp! Even fairly young children, however, do work out the basic notion of relativity to the class of objects under consideration: if asked to bring a small glass, they will bring a juice glass, not a twelve-ounce drinking glass, and if asked to bring a small spoon, they will bring a teaspoon rather than a tablespoon. The real difference from the adult senses of these terms appears when, having brought a juice glass, they are asked to bring a smaller one (e.g., a cordial glass): they may well bring another juice glass. They will also treat the comparative and noncomparative forms as freely substitutable, indicating that they partition each set of objects into big ones and small ones, and hence that one small one is as small as another. A third or a fourth term can be added to the partitioning, e.g., *tiny-baby* or *very-big*, but the principle remains the same—within the *tiny-baby* class, all things are equally *tiny-baby*. Donaldson and Wales (1970) found that children at this stage, when faced with two toy trees with a goodly number of apples hanging on each and asked which tree had more, will reply: "Both of them." The first step beyond this initial analysis of comparatives occurs when the child is able to give correct answers to questions like

> John is taller than Bill.
> Bill is taller than Pete.
> Who is the tallest?

A correct answer here indicates that the child has grasped the "transitivity" of the *taller* relation: younger children will often answer *Bill*, since they get two associations of *taller* (= *tall*, for them) with *Bill* but only one for *John* and *Pete*. The child has not reached the adult grasp of these constructions, however, until he is able to give the correct answer to

> John is taller than Bill.
> John is shorter than Pete.
> Who is the tallest?

(Even adults have to think an extra split-second.) What is involved here is the bringing into alignment as **inverses** the terms *shorter* and *taller*—i.e., the formation of the equivalence:

> X shorter than Y = Y taller than X.

Interestingly, full grasp of kinship terminology also depends on aligning *parent* and *child* as inverses and *brother/sister* as semireciprocals (with sex differentiation), and mastery of these constructions and terms only comes during the early primary-school years.

Picking out the relevant property of the noun which is modified by a dimension adjective also involves a lot of complicated knowledge. Manfred Bierwisch (1970, 1971) has sketched a componential analysis of the

relation of the terms *big, large/small; long/short; tall/short; (broad), wide/
narrow; thick/thin.* All of these have to do with "stretches" (extension)
along some dimension, but one must learn how to pick out which dimension
each adjective refers to. The dimension can be noted as a selectional restriction for each term:

$$long\ N: [Y_N\ \text{GREATER}\ Y\ \text{NORM}_N]\quad \langle Y\ \text{MAXIMAL EXTENSION}_N \rangle$$

This accounts for the anomaly of *long donut*: donuts are not thought of as
having a maximal extension. The linear dimension involved here is intuitively simpler than the triple dimension involved in *big/small*, which require the computation of volumes. Young children usually choose one size
adjective (usually *big*) and use it in an undifferentiated way, which might
be roughly paraphrased as 'having unusual extension (along any dimension)'
(Campbell and Wales, 1970; E. Clark, 1973)—only later do they differentiate *big* into *long, wide, thick*, etc. Piaget, Inhelder, and Szeminska
(1960: Chapter 14) note that the fully abstracted sense of *big* as 'volume'
is not established until 10 to 11 years: before that, children will be dis-
tracted by unusual length, height, or length of perimeter into judging a
"smaller" object as "larger" than another. There are also quirkier aspects of
the assignment of dimensional terms (*broad* vs. *wide; thick* vs. *deep*), and
it appears that even adults do not work out neat and consistent selectional
specifications for when to use *broad* and when *wide* (see the deliciously
vague and inconclusive Usage note for *broad* in the *AHD*).

One complexity of these dimensional terms that has not received
much attention is the difference between "stretches" and "spans," where
the latter is a distance between two points rather than the extension along
some physical parameter. For example, *high* and *tall* are differentiated in
this way:

> high cloud : tall building
> high telephone wires : tall telephone pole

One might speculate that span words, insofar as they express a relation
between things rather than some physically measurable dimension of objects, would be learned later than the parallel extension terms (for a brief
mention of evidence that this is so, see Clark, 1973: 93).

4.2

Duration Adverbials

The relations of adverbials to the things they modify are even more multi-
farious and complex than the relations of adjectives to nouns. Here I will
discuss only duration adverbials, but others (especially manner and extent)

are at least as complex. Just as the previous set of *ADJ-N* phrases show that *ADJ*s can modify different parts of a noun's sense, so the following set of sentences shows that adverbials of duration can modify predicates in different ways:

(1) He went to New York for two weeks.
(2) The rain stopped for two weeks.
(3) He passed away for two weeks.
(4) The tomato ripened for two weeks.

(1) is ambiguous over two readings: one may call the first the "duration-of-result" reading ('went to New York to stay for two weeks') and the other the "iterative" reading ('for two weeks made trips to New York'). (2) has only the first type of reading, (3) no reading at all (is anomalous), and (4) has a reading different from either of the first two sentences. How can this be?

The first sentence raises the phenomenon usually called "scope of modification." Since *go to N* entails *be at/in N subsequently*, one might paraphrase it as 'It came about that he was in New York' or in pidgin:

HE be IN NEW YORK COMES ABOUT

and then the duration-adverbial could be said to modify either the 'be in New York' part or the 'comes about' part:

For two weeks it came about that he was in New York.
It came about that for two weeks he was in New York.

This ambiguity, and the parallel ones involving *until*, are strong inducements to analyze GO TO as 'COME to be AT/IN', so that the duration-adverbial can always be said to modify a verb and the difference in scope can be traced to a difference in which of the *two* verbs is modified. This argument has been developed by the Chicago school of Generative Semantics (its history is reviewed in Green, 1974, but see note at end). A similar argument is based on the scope ambiguity of *nearly*:

He nearly went to N.Y. = 'but changed his mind'—'nearly left'
                        = 'but got off at Hoboken'—'went nearly to N.Y.'

Obviously the duration-of-result reading is possible only when some result is conceptually present—i.e., the verb is inchoative or causative. When it is an "activity," the reading is duration-of-activity only:

He read/shovelled snow for two hours.

Thus one can argue that inchoative and causative verbs should be represented as having an inchoative verb component such as COME ABOUT.

Since it is inchoative, *stop* in (2) has this duration-of-result reading, but it lacks the other, iterative reading. Why is this? An answer sketched by David Dowty (1972b) involves the assumption that the duration adverbial *for two weeks* involves the notion that what it modifies is true for all the time in the interval. This cannot be taken too literally, of course, since time returning from New York doesn't count against an iterative reading for (1), nor does time spent doing other things. One might say that the action must characterize the interval, though it is very difficult to pin this notion down further. In (1), the interval is long enough to allow several trips (probably), so 'repeated trips' is a possible way to characterize the interval and is a plausible reading. Notice that it disappears if *for two hours* is substituted, leaving (1) unambiguously duration-of-result like (2). In (2), the iterative reading seems to be blocked. Dowty suggests, not totally convincingly, that this is because for it to have stopped repeatedly it would have had to have started again, and this is incompatible with the assumption that 'no rain' characterizes the whole interval. Of course, something like (2'):

(2') The rain stopped at noon for two weeks.

is compatible with an iterative reading and hence is ambiguous as (1) is.

The same considerations block the iterative reading in (3). This is plainly out because 'passing away' is presumably something each individual does once only (but the iterative reading would, as usual, be possible in some fantasy world in which that factual assumption were lifted). (3) would also be ok if it had a plural subject, since 'instances of X pass away' could occur repeatedly:

(3') The victims passed away for two weeks.

The duration-of-result reading is implausible for a similar reason, though it is more clearly pragmatic (in the sense of Chapter VII): it seems odd to limit the duration-of-result to two weeks if one assumes it will last until the end of time. One can make this sort of consideration explicit:

?They cancelled his license irrevocably for two weeks.

The result of the blocking of both readings is an anomaly.

The fourth example does not have the iterative reading (you only ripen once if you're a tomato), and the duration-of-result is perhaps possible, though it takes a back seat the new sense. Like *go* and *pass away* and *stop, ripen* is inchoative, but the special aspect of its meaning is that, as noted in the Exercises in Chapter I and in previous chapters, it means 'become riper' (or 'go toward ripe' if we think of *ripe* as expressing an end-state—i.e., it, like *age* in Section 2.3, is a gradual Achievement). The point is that 'becoming riper (than it was)' is something that can be true for every instant in the interval. It is interesting to note that *turn* and *become* without the comparative form of the *ADJ* are not degree-inchoatives but Achievements: the duration-of-result reading is the only one likely:

The tomato turned/became ripe for two weeks (and then it turned rotten).

Clearly, duration adverbials are sensitive to the internal structure of verbs, and the problem of formalizing the rules that map the readings onto the sentences is very complex, involving universal quantifiers over time intervals, though, as noted, the universality must not be taken too strictly. Probably all time adverbials locating an event in or throughout an interval are more cognitively complex than those that locate events at points, since they involve some quantification of moments *t* rather than the simple pairing of an event with a moment. I know of no research on the acquisition of duration adverbials, but the complexity just mentioned may have a bearing on research that has been done concerning the acquisition of the connectives *before, after, when, while*, and *at the same time as*, which link two different actions or events as sequentially ordered or as simultaneous. Many have found that children find the simultaneous-event sentences hardest to handle (see Deborah Keller-Cohen, 1974, for a summary of research). Keller-Cohen found that sentences with *while* continued to pose difficulties for children even after they controlled *at the same time as*, which suggests that the extra complexity of the *while* relation—namely, that the duration of the second action may INCLUDE the duration of the first, not just be identical to it (though that is possible also)—may account for the difficulty. One of the trickier points of psycholinguistic research is picking out the parts of a semantic representation that do correlate with cognitive complexity, and one hopes that more precise and exact semantic representations will lead to the evaluation and design of research that is increasingly insightful.

Note on scope ambiguity with duration adverbials. Charles Fillmore (1974) suggests an alternative account of the scope ambiguity in sentences with duration adverbials in terms of "amalgamation rules" that fuse two sentences. The "go and remain" reading would be traced to two sentences:

He went to New York and he stayed there for two weeks.

He went to New York for two weeks.

Under such a treatment, scope ambiguities of this type would not reflect the internal structure of a single sentence (i.e., the "internal structure" of surface verbs), but the relation of ambiguity to type of verbs (i.e., that this ambiguity only occurs in the vicinity of an INCHOATIVE component) would appear as a condition on amalgamation of a sentence with *stay/re-*

main into the main sentence. It is hard to know what to make of this suggestion, however, until the amalgamation rules are written out.

READINGS FOR CHAPTER IV

Bolinger (1967) is a useful survey of types of adjectival modification, and his *Degree Words* (1972) is a study of gradability.

Verkuyl (1972) contains a great deal of interest on duration adverbials in English and Dutch, and Klooster (1972) deals with relative adjectives.

See König (1974) for a basic logic of temporal modifiers.

See Lawler (1974) for the use of "occasion" variables.

Dreyfuss et al. (1975) studied judgments of *cold* and *a long distance* in sentences with and without norm specifiers (*20° is cold/cold for Miami; 25 miles is a long distance/ a long distance to commute to work*). Interestingly, *cold* was treated, in the absence of a norm, as in relation to the weather, but no such assumed norm appeared for *a long distance*.

Bartsch and Vennemann (1972) give an explicit logic of relative adjectives.

EXERCISES AND PROBLEMS

1. What type of modification obtains in each of the italicized phrases?
   (a) These are *heavy dishes*.
   (b) Put the *healthy animals* in this pen.
   (c) Our *recent students* have had no trouble getting jobs.
   (d) Washington, Jefferson, and Jackson are among the *doubtful starters*.
   (e) The town has such *bad water* that everybody drinks beer.
   (f) He is a *slow learner*.

2. The duration adverbials *in a few minutes/hours/days* have a number of semantic peculiarities. With what type(s) of verbs do they occur and why are they not roughly equivalent to *in the night?*

3. Is there a scope ambiguity in
   (a) The letter almost went to Boston.
   (b) He didn't wake up until dawn.

4. How many and which readings do each of the following have (and why)?
   (a) The bread went stale for two weeks.
   (b) He went out of his mind for two years.

5. Do hedged noun phrases entail hedged components (typical bird → typical mammal)?

Semantic Roles

In many grammars of inflected languages such as Latin, Old English, Russian, German, or Finnish one finds the use of case inflections described in such terms as "ablative of Instrument," "dative of person affected," and "accusative of measure," and statements that the "doer of the action" is normally in the nominative case except when the sentence is passive, that the "thing affected" is in the accusative case, and so on. These are instructions about which case inflection to use when expressing certain relationships of nominals to the rest of the sentence, or, looked at the other way, how to interpret the role played by a participant that is referred to by a noun with a certain case. For example, in the Latin sentence

Parva formica onera magna ore trahit.

the first noun phrase (*parva formica* 'a small ant') is in the nominative case and hence identifiable as playing the role of "doer" of the action expressed by *trahit* ('carry'). The second phrase (*onera magna* 'great loads') is in the accusative case and identifiable as the thing affected by the action (i.e., it plays the Patient or "affected" role). The remaining noun (*ore* 'mouth') is in the ablative case, which is used (among other uses) to mark the role of Instrument.

In English, case inflections appear mainly on pronouns. In the sentence

> Her he lightly kissed upon the cheek.

we can identify *her* as the Patient and *he* as the "doer" even though we are deprived of the clue of word order normal for English. Roughly the same terms are useful for describing the "meanings" of case inflections in a wide variety of languages, though some languages make distinctions that others do not (there is, for example, an unusually rich set of cases having to do with location and movement in Finnish), and most languages allow some case inflections to indicate more than one semantic role, so that case inflection and role are not related one-to-one. Similar statements can be made concerning word order and the use of prepositions (or postpositions) in languages that lack case inflections. For example, if one wished to describe when to use the particle (postposition) *de* in Japanese as contrasted to *ni*, or the "dative" form of the article as contrasted to the accusative in German (following a preposition that allows either), or the "ablative" case ending in Latin where it can contrast with the "accusative," or the "locative" case in Turkish versus the "dative," or *in* versus *(in)to* in English, one would find it useful to say that the nouns of the first column are understood as "place-at-which," and those of the second as "place-to-which," or as Locations as opposed to Goals:

Japanese:	*rooka de hasiru* hallway in run		*rooka ni hasiru* hallway to run
German:	*lehren auf der Universität* teach at the university		*gehen auf die Universität* go to the university
Latin:	*in castris erimus* in camp we-will-be		*in castra venimus* to camp we-will-go
Turkish:	*sandalye-de oturuyordum* chair-in I-was-sitting		*sandalye-ye oturdum* chair-onto I sat

This is just a sample of languages that, though they use different means, signal what seems to be the same conceptual difference. The term **semantic role** will be used to refer to conceptual relations of this nature, though some writers use the term "deep case," which unfortunately is easy to confuse with the morphological case inflections: the point is that languages have systematic ways of marking semantic roles ("deep cases"), but not all of them employ case inflections (surface or morphological cases) to do this.

Certain roles keep turning up in the grammars of diverse languages, and in recent years a number of linguists have tried to define a basic set of semantic roles that might be useful in the description of all languages. Different writers have defined the roles slightly differently, or have revised their earlier descriptions, with the result that there is something less than general agreement about how to describe the roles played by nominals in a goodly number of sentences. Some have supposed that this is simply a problem of definition and hence that it will be possible eventually to define each role precisely, so that everyone will be able to agree on the proper assignment of roles. This seems fundamentally mistaken to me: these concepts have each a central core or prototype that most analysts would agree to and a number of associated properties, but they have fringes and overlappings with the fringes of other roles where a decision to assign one role instead of another will inevitably be somewhat arbitrary.

Table I illustrates the degree of variation in the assignment of roles by various analysts in what all would agree are basic sentences of English. Two things are likely to strike the reader's eye on first examination: one is the complete agreement about the role of *window* in (3) and (4), which may seem odd; the second is the amount of variation in (6) through (10), which is not merely terminological (as it largely is in [13]). Some of the reasons for the decisions reflected on the chart will emerge as the roles are considered one by one.

5.1

Agent

Although there is general agreement that *John* is the Agent in (1), a number of slightly different definitions lead to different classifications of the Subject in such sentences as

(i) John sneezed.
(ii) John accidentally ran over a cat.
(iii) John floated down the river to escape the soldiers.
(iv) The wind blew the table over.
(v) The rolling boulder crushed my petunias.
(vi) Loss of blood killed the victim.

Charles Fillmore usually defines Agent as 'instigator of the action'. This is nicely vague with respect to whether the Agent intends to perform the action. Intentionality is taken as definitional for Agents by some writers (e.g., Quirk et al., 1972: 353 note b; Jackendoff, 1972: 32). If intentionality is definitional for Agents, then the Subjects of (i), (ii), (iv), (v), and (vi) are not Agents. Chafe (1970: 109) takes the notion of self-energy source as the definitional component rather than intent, so that (iv) would have an Agent Subject for him, probably also (ii). Further, he suggests that objects which make things happen because of their position or momentum be considered to have "derived potency" and hence to be "energy sources" for the event—

Table I

	Quirk et al.[a]	Fillmore-I[b]	Chafe	Fillmore-II[c]	Anderson
(1) *John* broke the window with a stone.	agent	Agent	Agent	Agent	erg
(2) John broke the window *with a stone*.	instrument	Instrument	Instrument	Instrument	?
(3) John broke *the window* with a stone.	affected	Objective	Patient	Object	nom
(4) *The window* broke.	affected	Objective	Patient	Object	nom
(5) The book is *in the study*.	locative	Locative	Location	Location	loc
(6) They sent a wire *to Washington*.	locative	Locative	Location	Goal	loc
(7) They gave the prize *to Mary*.	recipient	Dative	Beneficiary	Goal	loc
(8) *Mary* has the prize.	recipient	Dative	Beneficiary	Location	loc
(9) He washed the floor *for Mary*.	recipient	Benefactive	Beneficiary	Goal	?loc
(10) *John* saw the ghost.	recipient	Dative	Experiencer	Experiencer	loc
(11) He made a car *out of soap*.	—	—	—	Source	abl
(12) It fell *off the table*.	—	—	—	Source	abl
(13) He made *a car* out of soap.	effected	Factitive	Complement	Goal	nom

[a] Quirk et al. (1972) is basically a development of Halliday (1967–68).
[b] Fillmore-I is the model in Fillmore (1968) adopted in Stockwell et al. (1973), where *neutral* is used for Objective.
[c] Fillmore-II is the sketch given in Fillmore (1971).

thus, (v) would have an Agent Subject. Cruse (1973) calls this subtype of "doer" "effective." The element of animacy is usually held to be associated but not definitional, though of course it would be entailed for those who take the intentional view. Obviously, being animate accounts for being capable of being a self-energy source. The verb *sneeze* raises problems, since the Subject is the self-energy source, but the "action" is (presumably) involuntary (i.e., not controllable)—at least in some instances. Various people scruple at calling *sneeze* an action, though if one takes self-energy source strictly, it must have an Agent Subject (see Cruse, 1973; Dillon, 1974).

How is one to view all of this? Nilsen (1973) and Cruse (1973) have suggested that the notion of Agent is not semantically primitive but can be analyzed into a number of components. Nilsen uses the analysis to claim that only one set of components properly defines Agent, though one "component" for him is the possibility of being regarded as intentional. Cruse argues that the notion of "doer" can be broken down into four roles, only one of which is Agent proper (the others are effective, volitive, and initiative). It is conceivable that there is no right or wrong definition of an Agent, particularly if one is trying to capture the conceptualizations people actually make and use, but rather that Agent is vague in the way that *cup* is vague. One might also speculate, along lines suggested by Ingram (1971) and Bowerman (1973), that children only gradually abstract the more general characterization from such parts as "the role played by the understood Subject of imperatives," "the one who makes things happen," "the one who gets blamed for something," and so on. The refinements would come in the direction of including some inanimates, recognizing limitations of intention and voluntary control, and the like, and adults might be expected to have carried out these refinements in different ways. It should be noted that this view was NOT held at least by Fillmore in the heyday of nativism (1968: 24): "The case notions comprise a set of universal, presumably innate, concepts which identify certain types of judgments human beings are capable of making about the events that are going on around them, judgments about such matters as who did it, who it happened to, and what got changed."

5.2

Instrument

Instrument pairs with Agent in most systems. Most case grammarians would agree with the characterization of *with a stone* in (2) as an Instrument, but again definitions lead to different classifications of the italicized nominals:

(i) *The key* opened the lock.
(ii) The boy died *from loss of blood.*

(iii) *The ball* broke the window.
(iv) John accidentally cut himself *with a razor blade*.
(v) *Seeing Mary* reminded John of his wife's birthday.
(vi) *The rock* jammed the machine.   He stopped the train
                                        with his body.

Some would take the notion "thing used to perform an action" as definitional for Instrument. The notion of "thing" commits one to the concrete-
ness of the Instrument, so *loss of blood* in (ii) and *seeing Mary* in (v) would
not be Instruments. "Use" seems to commit one to there being an intentional Agent about, so *the razor blade* in (iv) would not be an Instrument.
Depending on how strongly one insisted on the presence of an implied
Agent, one might have reservations about *the rock* in (vi) or *the ball* in
(iii). Chafe (1970: 155) suggests that they are Agents; Cruse (1973) suggests
that the sentences are ambiguous over an instrument reading ('someone
succeeded in breaking the window with the ball') and an "effective" reading ('because, flying in that direction, the ball broke the window'). Fillmore
originally defined Instrument as 'thing used' but subsequently redefined
Instrument as 'immediate cause', which allows both abstract and nonagen-
tive Instruments. Hence all of these sentences would contain Instruments
for him. Alternatively, one could define a separate role—Huddleston (1970)
calls it Force—for things where no ulterior Agent is understood, retaining
Instrument for cases where an Agent is present.

It may appear that the definition of roles is intuitionism run wild.
Case grammarians commonly invoke two rules of thumb to decide whether
two nominals are of the same role (though not to determine which role they
are):

A. Each nominal in a simple sentence plays a different role (except for
   prepositional phrases that successively narrow down a location:

   It was in the basement behind the washing machine under a box.

   On these, see Bennett, 1975.)

B. Unlike roles cannot be conjoined (without humorous effect).

The oddity of   better : a puff of wind

   ?The wind blew the table over with its gusts.

could be traced to a violation of (A) and used to argue that *the wind* is an
Instrument (hence, we cannot have a second Instrument *with its gusts*).
Perhaps the tendency to "personify" *the wind* here could be traced to the
presence of *with its gusts*: if there is an Instrument, *the wind* must be an
Agent. Since the following is ok,

   He filled the tank with gasoline with a hose.

one could argue that *with gasoline* is not an Instrument but some other relation (?Substance). The second rule of thumb (B) could be used to argue that *John* and *a stone* must play different roles, as must *loss of blood* and *the bullet*:

> ?John and a stone broke the window.
> ?The bullet and loss of blood killed the victim.

Unfortunately, the evidence of these tests is not always clear-cut, and other constraints may be involved in the perception of oddity. To be sure, the role of a nominal will have to do with the prepositions or case endings (or both) that it occurs with: the "typical" preposition occurring with an Instrument is *with* (unless the Instrument is abstract), but others are possible (*on, of, from*), and no one morphological or syntactic trait is sufficient to discriminate roles conclusively. One can say of the following set

> (a) He was killed by a piece of glass.
> (b) He was killed with a piece of glass.
> (c) He cut himself with a piece of glass.
> (d) He cut himself on a piece of glass.

that (b) suggests an ulterior Agent more strongly than (a) and that (c) is more likely to be used to describe (deliberate) self-injury than (d). These judgments raise rather advanced problems connected with the notion that these prepositions mark roles without contributing content of their own— i.e., that their "role-marking" sense is entirely distinct from their other, more spatial senses.

5.3

A f f e c t e d / P a t i e n t / O b j e c t

The decision to treat the Direct Objects of most transitive verbs and the Subjects of some intransitives as expressing the same semantic role seems one of the odder aspects of case grammars. One is inclined to view the former as "acted upon" (hence the term *affected*) but the latter as "undergoing change" or simply as "described." Most case grammarians stretch the concept of Patient even further by classifying the Subjects of most adjectival, adverbial, and nominal predicates as members of this role:

> John is fat.
> John is in the bathroom.
> John is a Mormon.

It appears strange for a model that sets out to describe semantic bases for morphological and syntactic facts to group some Direct Objects and some Subjects as members of the same role. There are languages, however, in which one case ending is used for all of these nominals (the "absolutive" case) and another for Agents (the "ergative" case). These ergative (or ergative-absolutive) languages include Eskimo, Basque, Avar, and certain aborigine languages of Australia.

Ergative languages appear to be of two types, differing with respect to the marking of intransitive verbs with Agents (*cough, walk, yawn, burp, bark, twinkle, shine*—that is to say, the verbs translating these in the languages). Some languages (Dakota, Iroquoi languages generally [Chafe, 1970: 232], and Georgian) place the Subjects of the equivalent verbs in the ergative (Agent) case, but other languages (Chinook, Basque, Avar) treat the subjects as "absolutive" (the Patient case). The inflectional marking in these latter languages can be said to be less transparent semantically, since the "Patient" case is used for some Agents. (It should be mentioned that languages of the latter type are commonly said to exhibit the "true" ergative pattern.) The proper generalization would seem to be that some languages mark Agents by one case and Patients by another more consistently than others. Languages do change in regard to the semantic transparency of their case marking. Martin Harris (1975) gives an interesting account of how Latin came to be less transparent.

The main point of disagreement between case grammarians in regard to Patient has to do with the classification of animates. In his earlier sketch of case grammar, Fillmore gave considerable weight to animacy and chose to classify the italicized nominals in

> The criminal murdered *the girl*.
> *She* died.

as Datives ("of person affected") rather than as Patients ("Objects"). This decision he has subsequently abandoned. Instead, he has proposed a separate role called Experiencer for "psychological verbs." The italicized nominals would be Experiencers for Fillmore (also Chafe):

> John scared *Mary*.
> *Mary* likes eggplant.

Presumably an animate Direct Object of *burn* would also be classified as an Experiencer (unless the Direct Object is understood to be 'person's body'), though an inanimate would be classified as Object (Patient).

5.4

Location (and Source and Goal)

The source of the variation in the analyses of (6) through (10) in Table I is the differing views taken of possession, location, and direction.

    (5) The book is *in the study*.
    (6) They sent a wire *to Washington*.
    (7) They gave the prize *to Mary*.
    (8) *Mary* has the prize.
    (9) He washed the floor *for Mary*.
  (10) *John* saw the ghost.

There is virtual agreement about (5). The question in (6) concerns whether a separate role should be set up for "Place to which something goes," which, as noted in the introduction, takes a different case in various languages from that of simple location and takes different prepositions in English (*to* versus *at/in*). Fillmore chooses to do so; the others rely on the semantic characterization of the verb as a verb of motion to predict this reinterpretation of Location. This is primarily a notational difference, since one could define "verb of motion" as a nonstative verb that occurs with Source and Goal. In (8), the difference in analyses has to do with animacy again, with the systems of the first three columns giving more weight to the possession by an animate being of something than to the location of the thing with the being. This view of the special status of an involved animate being extends to (9), though Fillmore-I sets up a special role here ("Benefactive"). This relation is even extended to (10) for the writers who do not establish a separate Experiencer role for "psychological verbs."

    Sentences (11) through (13) again have to do with motion:

  (11) He made a car *out of soap*.
  (12) It fell *off the table*.
  (13) He made *a car* out of soap.

Those who have a distinct Goal role usually also have a Source role that *off the table* in (12) would illustrate. Indeed, as noted above, some would treat all "motion" sentences in terms of Source/Goal pairs, one of which might be unspecified. In (12) it would be a Goal like *onto the floor*. Sentences (11) and (13) have to do with verbs of creating. In (11), *out of soap*, being marked with a typical Source preposition *out of*, has the look of a Source and would be paired, in Anderson's system, with an understood Goal ("into existence"). *A car* in (13) is peculiar in that it comes into existence as a result of the action of the verb. Some therefore prefer not to call it Patient but to create another role for it ("Factitive").

5.5

Other Roles (and When to Stop)

Fillmore and others have suggested additional roles that seem distinct from those listed so far. Among these are the roles of the italicized phrases in

John ran out the door *down the steps* into the street. (Path)
John robbed a bank *with a friend*. (Comitative)
He struggled *against the habit*. (Counteragent)

and some writers would include adverbials of Means, Extent, Reason, and Purpose as semantic roles:

It runs *on electricity*. (Means)
He ran *two miles.* ⎫
It cost *two dollars.* ⎬ (Extent)
He did it *for/out of love*. (Reason)
He did it *to gain attention*. (Purpose)

There is probably some tension between the particular specifications imposed by certain verbs on the nominals associated with them and the general role-types they could be classified under, and also between the role and the inherent components of the nominal. This latter tension has already been noted in regard to animacy. Nilsen (1973) identifies the following italicized nominals by what appear to be their inherent components rather than their roles as characterized by the verbs *push* and *like*:

He is pushing *the lawnmower* now. (Instrument—p. 130)
I like *Paris* better than Berlin. (Location—p. 131)

Chapin (1972) finds the following analyses in Stockwell et al. (1972) surprising:

He aimed *the gun* at her. (Instrument)
They filled *the pool* with water. (Location)

since *gun* and *pool* seem to be "acted upon" (= Patient). Perhaps, as suggested above, one should view the "mistakes" of others simply as data concerning their intuitions as speakers. I will return to this at the end. Partly, the uncertainty has to do with how one analyses the sense of the verb. Should we say that the Direct Object of *paint* is a Goal or a Patient (*paint* X : PUT PAINT ON X); should we say the Indirect Object of *give* is Goal (CAUSE Direct Object to GO to Indirect Object) or Locative (CAUSE Indirect Object to HAVE Direct Object)?

5.6

Subjects and Objects

The only case inflection on nouns in modern English is the genitive: semantic roles correlate with syntactic function and with prepositions. That is, there are generalizations to be made about which roles turn up as Subjects, which Direct Objects, and which Oblique Objects (i.e., objects of prepositions) parallel to those to be made about which turn up in the ablative or accusative or nominative case in inflected languages. Concentrating only on Agent, Instrument, Patient, Location (and Source and Goal), we can make the following general statement concerning what will be Subject:

Agent > Instrument > Patient > Location

which can be read as: 'If there is an Agent, it becomes Subject; if not, but there is an Instrument, it becomes Subject; if neither, Patient becomes Subject'. When an Agent or Instrument is Subject, the Patient is normally the Direct Object; if an Agent is Subject, Instrument is usually an Oblique Object with *with*; Location is usually an Oblique Object:

John broke the window with a stick.
AGT   PAT   INS

The stick broke the window.
INS   PAT

The window broke.
PAT

In passive sentences the Patient is "promoted" to Subject, and the Agent or Instrument is demoted to an Oblique Object (of *by* or *with*) and the verb is "marked").

The window was broken with a stick by John.
PAT   INS   AGT

Since Location is at the bottom of the Subject hierarchy, it would become Subject only if there were no other candidate. This may be the case in

The room is hot. (= It is hot in the room.)

There are verbs that allow, or require, a Location as Subject, however:

(1) The can contains/holds water.
(2) The house got a coat of paint.   (here Subj = Goal)
(3) The tree lost its leaves.   (here Subj = Source)

and there are verbs that allow or require a Location as Direct Object:

(4) John reached St. Louis. ⎫
        entered the room. ⎬ (Goal)
(5) John left St. Louis. (Source)
(6) Smoke filled the room. (Location)
(7) John gave Bill a cold. ⎫
        owes Bill five dollars. ⎬ (Goal)

John Anderson (1971) proposes that these unusual placements of roles be treated as arising from "secondary" role assignments—i.e., that the Locations are also regarded as Patients or Agents, picking up the second role by being made Subject or Direct Object. Thus in (4) through (7) the Location nominals are also understood to play Patient roles, and this can be extended to (1) through (3) if one assumes a Pat/Loc is higher on the Subject hierarchy than a simple Patient. Anderson calls attention to the following set:

(8) The performance was pleasing to John.
      PAT   LOC

(9) John was pleased with the performance.
     LOC/PAT   PAT

(10) The performance pleased John.
     AGT/PAT   LOC/PAT

(11) John was pleased by the performance.   (passive of 10)
    LOC/PAT   AGT/PAT

(12) John liked the performance.   (same as 9)
    LOC/PAT   PAT

Where (8) would be the usual case, (9) would involve regarding *John* as a Patient as well as a Loc (hence the notation Loc/Pat) and (10) would involve that with the additional view of the *performance* as an Agent (or Instrument—a causative force of John's response). (Whether *John* is called Loc or Experiencer is immaterial.) It is clear from this set that assignment of a secondary role affects the view taken of the situation. This shading may approach a difference of entailments. Georgia Green (1974) argues that (13) is contradictory but (14) is not:

(13) I teach the little monsters arithmetic, but they never learn it.
(14) I teach arithmetic to the little monsters, but they never learn it.

One might trace this difference to the effects of the secondary Patient characterization given to *monsters* in (13): they are understood as changed by the action of teaching (hence: they learn), and similarly for

(15) ?I showed Jane the error but she didn't see it.
(16) I showed the error to Jane but she didn't see it.

In many cases, however, the shading is virtually imperceptible (see Chapter I, Section 1.3):

(17) He gave Mary a ring./He gave a ring to Mary.
(18) John fought Harry./John fought with Harry.

where the difference is slight at most. It should be mentioned that Green regards the differences between (13) and (14) and between (15) and (16) as predictable from different senses that the verbs have in each sentence (though not for 17 and 18). For *teach* these are roughly:

(13) *teach*$_1$: Subj CAUSE Indirect Obj to LEARN Direct Obj
               BY TEACHING Direct Obj

(14) *teach*$_2$: Subj INTENDING Indirect Obj to LEARN Direct Obj
Subj TEACH Direct Obj

and Fillmore takes a similar position for *load* and *smear* (see Chapter I, Exercise 12). What makes this a subtle and difficult matter is that the borderline between shading and actual differences of entailment is not easy to discern. It does seem clear, however, that different senses of words will have different options with respect to Direct Objects: Green (1974: 82–84) points out that *give* with the sense 'provide with' requires "objectivalization" of the Goal:

Mary gave John pneumonia./?Mary gave pneumonia to John.
Mary gave John a piece of her mind./?Mary gave a piece of her mind to
John.

A similar difference has been noted between (19) and (20):

(19) The garden swarmed with bees.
(20) Bees swarmed in the garden.

where (19) is more likely to give rise to the picture of bees all over the garden than (20), though this can perhaps be attributed to (19) being regarded as a statement characterizing the garden, while (20) is a statement locating the bees. In any case, one can note that, whatever deeper facts may account for it, occurrence as a Direct Object is associated with the notion of Patienthood, and, to a slighter degree, occurrence as a Subject with Agenthood.

It is possible to regard certain verbs (*have, use, get*) as useful for creating unusual Subjects or Direct Objects:

(21) He had a car run over him.
(22) The wall has a picture on it.
(23) He used a stick to break the window.

(21) is actually ambiguous over a reading where *he* is understood as Agent ('arranged an "accident" ') and one where *he* is not ('suffered an accident'). These are touched on in Fillmore (1968) and Dillon (to appear).

A further advantage to the notion of double roles is that one can show the relation between *buy* and *sell, lend* and *borrow*, etc., in terms of the basic roles Patient, Source, and Goal, where each verb picks out either the Source or the Goal as Agent.

5.7

Other Uses of Case Grammar

As presented here, case grammar is a way of describing certain facts and of making certain generalizations about the facts. Certainly the facts it describes can be described in other ways, and there are many facts that it does not describe very well, or at all. It has nonetheless been suggestive to people working in the acquisition of language and in derivational morphology. To take the latter first: Lees (1970) among others has noted that various compound types can be described in case terms very succinctly: e.g., the *ash tray* type as Pat-Goal, the *oil well* type as Pat-Source; and of course the *-er* suffix can be described as the Agentive or Instrumental suffix, *-ee*, as a Patient-of-verb suffix. One can also observe that the *self-* prefix is restricted to Agentive verbs—i.e.,

He cut himself.

is only *self-injury* if *he* is understood as Agent. A far more elaborate development of Lee's suggestive sketch can be found in Kastovsky (1973).

For some time psycholinguists have been interested in the case analysis of children's first two- and three-word utterances, because most of them are interpretable in terms of Pat + Loc, Agt + Pat, and so on, giving the impression that children assume these notions as given or obvious: that is, their grammars appear to be organized in this way. Fairly enthusiastic applications of case analysis to the data of child speech can be found in Brown (1971) and Slobin (1971), and Brown (1973) is a more searching but still optimistic survey. Methodological problems are involved, however, in that the fact that adults interpret children's utterances this way is not much of a guarantee that the child is employing anything like the adult conceptions of the roles. Research currently underway may sharpen the claims being made.

In this brief sketch of case grammars I have emphasized the intuitive basis of semantic roles. Some case grammarians might object to this emphasis and maintain that the roles may form a part of the competence of speakers to which they might have only partial conscious access. On this view, one could hope to arrive at "correct" definitions that would enable one to ignore the mistakes of other case grammarians and the erratic intuitions of one's informants (and oneself). This interpretation would make case grammar a more respectable basis for a generative grammar but, I think, would deprive it of most of its interest.

READINGS FOR CHAPTER V

On ergative languages see Anderson (1971) or Lyons (1968), also Anderson on local cases in Finnish.

On Comitative, see Walmsley (1971) and Buckingham (1973).

On Force and abstract "Agents" see Huddleston (1970), Babcock (1972), and Lee (1969, 1971a, b).

A detailed study of the usefulness of case grammar in analyzing early "sentences" of child speech in several languages is Bowerman (1973). Brown's (1973) discussion includes Bowerman's results.

Adams (1973) uses semantic roles to describe patterns of word formation.

Bennett (1975) is an advanced but very interesting study of expressions of location and movement in English.

EXERCISES AND PROBLEMS

1. Identify the roles played by the italicized *NPs* and *PPs*:
    (a) *John* shrugged.
    (b) John kissed *Mary*.
    (c) Mary sliced the dough *with a wire*.
    (d) Max cleaned *the silverware*.
    (e) John told *Mary* about the accident.
    (f) *The water* spurted *from the pipe*.

2. Each of the following is ambiguous over two readings, which differ in the role assigned to a nominal. Describe the two readings in terms of the roles.
    (a) John rose.
    (b) This coat is warm.
    (c) John made her a milkshake.
    (d) John bumped his head on the rafters.
    (e) John smelled the cabbage.

3. Do you perceive a difference in meaning between (a) and (b)? If so, should this be described as a difference of role assignment, or secondary role assignment?
    (a) He pressed the doorbell with his cane.
    (b) He pressed his cane on the doorbell.

4. What problems does the italicized expression pose for the system of analysis given here?
    She wore a green dress *to the party*.

5. Discuss the differences of meaning between each of the pairs:
    (a) 1. They planted trees in the garden.
        2. They planted the garden with trees.

    (b) 1. The ground was strewn with litter.
        2. Litter was strewn on the ground.

    (c) 1. A flash accompanied the explosion.
        2. The explosion was accompanied with/by a flash.

Negatives, Quantifiers, and Connectives in Logic and Language

One of the surest ways to fail a course in symbolic logic is to assume that the symbols introduced ('∨', '&', '→', '∃', '∀') stand for the words *or, and, if, some,* and *all* and can be translated by them one-for-one. One would have to be half asleep to make this mistake, since most texts and teachers stress that the units and combinatorial rules ("syntax") of symbolic logic constitute an artificial language whose relation to English is often somewhat obscure. Its very independence of English makes it useful as a means of describing the logical properties of sentences of English. We can, for example, express the "ambiguity" of

> We must operate today or the patient will die.

(i.e., whether we think the operation will prevent death or not—"I didn't say he would live if we operated, only that he won't if we don't") in terms of whether "inclusive" or "exclusive" *or* (∨ or ∧) is present, and similarly we can express the relatedness of the following sentences:

> If the red light flashes, the machine is out of whack.
> When the red light flashes, the machine is out of whack.

by saying that *if* and *when* both have the sense of the entailment connective →. As the logical complexity of sentences increases, the usefulness of a formal, nonverbal notation also increases. There are actually a number of different formal logics—if one is interested in articulating the logical structure of English sentences, one may choose one or another or suggest modifications in existing ones to capture the logical properties. The representation—whichever one selects—of the logical form of a sentence is in some sense psychologically real, since speakers are able to compute the logical properties of sentences: some such computation underlies such claims as "that doesn't follow," "that's not true," and so on. How speakers are able to compute the logical properties of sentences is obviously an important question—and one under intensive study. In this chapter I will attempt only to suggest the kinds of phenomena that an adequate model must elucidate. There is another essentially psychological matter: often not all of the logically possible readings of sentences are equally likely to occur to speakers —there appear to be contextual and pragmatic considerations that suppress certain readings in particular instances. The three general topics to be considered are those central to any introductory course in logic: negatives, quantifiers, and connectives.

6.1

Negatives

In Chapter I we defined logical equivalence of sentences as truth over the same range of situations, or, we might say, compatibility with the same states of affairs. The logical treatment of simple sentence negation is a little surprising at first, because it says that the logical form of

John kissed Mary.

is

$((JOHN(x))$ & $(MARY(y))$ & $(KISSED(x, y)))$
One is called John and one is called Mary and he kissed her

The negation of this sentence is equivalent to

(1)   John didn't kiss Mary: $(-(JOHN(x))$ ∨ $-(MARY(y))$ ∨
$$-(KISSED\ (x,\ y)))$$
       x isn't called John or y isn't called Mary or they didn't kiss
       (or some or all or these) ['∨' symbolizes inclusive *or*; '−' = *not*].

This formula is compatible with seven distinguishable situations:

     (a)   One kissed one called Mary, but he wasn't called John.
     (b)   One called John kissed one, but she wasn't called Mary.

(c) One called John and one called Mary were not in a kissing relation.
(d) One kissed one, but he wasn't John and she wasn't Mary.
(e) One is called John, but he didn't kiss one and she wasn't called Mary.
(f) One is called Mary, but she wasn't kissed by one and he wasn't called John.
(g) One wasn't John, one wasn't Mary, and he didn't get into a kissing relation with her.

The point is that if at least one of the conditions for the truth of *John kissed Mary* is false, the whole statement is. (1) could be said to be ambiguous over the seven situations it is compatible with. In practice, of course, (c) seems the likeliest reading, but (a), (b), and (d) can be induced by contrastive stress (and special intonation) (indicated by capitals):

(a) = JOHN didn't kiss Mary.
(b) = John didn't kiss MARY.
(d) = JOHN didn't kiss MARY.

The more material there is in the sentence, the more ways there are of failing to be true:

(2)   John didn't kiss Mary gallantly on the cheek.

Here the failure of two more things could account for the *not*: he kissed her gallantly, but not on the cheek; he kissed her on the cheek, but not gallantly.

Matters are more complicated, however, because negation can also operate over the individual components within a word. Thus,

(3)   John didn't murder Mary.

is compatible not only with seven states of affairs parallel to the kissing sentence (1), but also to situations where

—he killed her, but he didn't mean to.
—she died, but he didn't cause it.
—he tried to, but she didn't die.

(and combinations, as before), where what is being negated is the INTENTIONAL component of *murder* in the first, the CAUSE component in the second, and the DIE component in the third alternative. Similarly,

(4)   Leslie isn't a bachelor.

could be true because Leslie is not MALE, or because MARRIED, or because NOT ADULT. It is evident that the number of readings a sentence can have when it is negated provides a clue to the components internal to words. One possible interpretation of (3) is the 'did it, but didn't mean to' reading, but one can imagine situations in which this would not be so—if, for example, (3) were spoken by a doctor coming out of the Intensive Care

Unit in a hospital: "Book him for aggravated assault." Similarly, (4) would most likely be taken in isolation as involving a claim that Leslie is married, but suppose someone says to Leslie's recently divorced father (he having been granted custody of Leslie), "How does it feel to be two bachelors kicking around the house?" Father might then reply, "Leslie isn't a bachelor, he's still only eight." It has been said that the likeliest reading is somehow semantically marked by calling the less-likely-to-be-negated components "presupposed to be true," but Ruth Kempson (1975) argues along the lines sketched here that this is simply a matter of what information is shared, and assumed to be shared, by Speaker and Hearer when the sentence is uttered.

There are cases where an element can be understood to be negated only when it is to the right of the negative:

(5)   John doesn't beat his wife because he loves her.
(6)   Because he loves her, John doesn't beat his wife.

The first sentence can be true either of the (a) or (b) situations:

> (a) He beats her, but for some other reason.
> (b) He doesn't beat her—that's because he loves her.

The sentence can be false because the reason given is incorrect—i.e., the *because* clause can be the negated element. This is not true for (6), which has only the (b) reading, where the *because* clause stands to the left of the negative. This seems to be true for adverbial elements that can be optionally shifted to the front of the sentence. Even at the front, of course, the adverbial can be negated if the negative precedes it:

> Not because he loves her does he beat her.

Evidently the position of the negative element in the sentence has something to do with what it can be understood to negate, but the precise statement of the relationship is still somewhat elusive.

A curious fact about negation is that a noun phrase to the right of the *not* can optionally be understood to be negated with the sense 'there does not exist any individual referred to by this phrase'. Thus,

(7)   John didn't kiss a girl.

can be taken to mean that he kissed no girls, as well as that there was a girl he didn't kiss. This 'no girls' reading tends to disappear (though it can remain if stressed) when *a girl* is moved to the left of the negative:

(8)   A girl wasn't kissed by John.

Ray Jackendoff (1972) and Manfred Bierwisch (1971) link this phenomenon to the fact that noun phrases following certain verbs such as *want*, *look for*, and *ask for* can also be optionally understood as not referring to a specific individual. These are said in logic to be "referentially opaque" environments:

(9)   John is looking for a girl.

(9) can be understood either as a search for a particular girl (in which case one can continue: I hope he finds *her*—this is the "transparent" reading) or as a search for any old girl (in which case: I hope he finds *one*—the opaque reading). (This phenomenon is discussed under the heading *random* in Chafe [1970].) Intuitively, the link would seem to be that for opaque contexts, any one you find will be ok; for *not*, any one you try will fail. Note, however, that this interpretation is optional, as it is with *look for, want*, etc. There is also the difference that with the verbs, the opaque reading is possible even when the object is shifted to the left of the verb—this is not true, we have seen, for *not*:

   It's a girl John's looking for—not a wife.

6.2

Quantifiers

One entailment passed over in the preceding account is that noun phrases usually entail the existence of the thing or things they refer to (referentially opaque environments excepted). The entailment corresponds to the existential quantifier ∃ of quantificational logic. Quantification is not possible with proper names (since, when used as proper names, they entail the existence of a unique referent, not "some" referent). We can add quantification by replacing *John* with *a boy* and Mary with *a girl*:

$$\exists x\, \exists y\, ((\text{BOY}(x))\ \&\ (\text{GIRL}(y))\ \&\ (\text{KISS}(x,\ y)))$$

which can be translated roughly 'there exists one that is a boy and there exists one that is a girl such that he kissed her'. This is not quite right as a translation, for '∃' is usually translated 'at least one'. This formula will be true each time there is some boy who kisses some girl, and it will be true if there are more than one of each involved. Thus this formula could be translated as either

A boy kissed a girl.

or

Some boys kissed some girls.

To take simpler cases with only one indefinite singular noun phrase:

(10) Someone is crying.
      $\exists x(CRY(x))$ = There is one that is crying.
(11) A child is crying.
      $\exists x(CHILD(x))$ & $(CRYING(x))$ = There is one that is a child and that is
                                        crying.

(*A/an* could be called a quantifier here—it has been traced historically to *one*.) There are, of course, many quantifiers in English (*few, a lot, many, several, some, one, two*, etc.), most of which have not attracted much attention from logicians, but *all* and *every* have, because they appear to translate the symbol '∀' [or '(x)']. This symbol would be used to formulate the meaning of *all* in

(12) All the children were crying. $\forall x((CHILD(x)) \rightarrow (CRYING(x)))$

This reads: 'For all x, if x is a child, x is crying'. The entailment arrow appears instead of the 'and' (&) because we can infer from (12) that if something is not crying, it is not a child. There does not seem to be much difference in truth-value between (12) and (13):

(13) Every child was crying.

and one might conclude that *all* is logically equivalent with *every*. There is a shading of difference in meaning, where *every* suggests a check of each child—it might be said to have the component DISTRIBUTED which *all* does not have. This component does not seem to affect its truth-value here, but as we shall see, this is not always true.

    Similar to (12) and (13) is the "generic" sentence (14):

(14) Children cry.

(Note the tense of the verb is simple present, not progressive. The past of a generic is *used to* or *would always*.) This sentence does not refer to a particular state of affairs but is a statement of "general truth." It should be obvious that (14) is not logically equivalent to (12) or (13), since a tearless child here and there does not make (14) false, since it only says they generally do cry. Some have proposed a new symbol to represent this quantifier; others use ∀ with a warning that it is not the same as the '∀' of *all*.

Let us return to sentences with explicit quantifiers to see how *every* and *all* differ. (15) has two possible readings, represented by the diagrams (a) and (b):

(15)   All the boys kissed a girl.

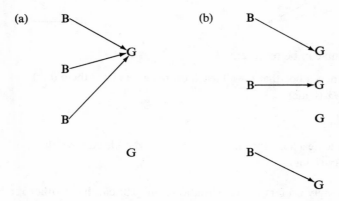

The (a) reading can be represented:

(a) There is a girl that all who were boys kissed.
$\exists y \ \forall x \ ((BOY(x) \ \& \ GIRL(y)) \rightarrow (KISS(x, y)))$

The (b) reading:

(b) For all who were boys there was a girl that they kissed.
$\forall x \ \exists y \ ((same))$

(The translation is unidiomatic—more naturally 'For each who was a boy ...'.) The difference in logical form is called a difference of **scope** of the quantifiers: $\forall$ is said to have narrow scope in (a), wide scope in (b). Now consider (16):

(16)   Every boy kissed a girl.

For me, (16) has only the (b) reading, or strongly prefers it. We can then say that the difference of *every* and *all* is that *every* favors the wide-scope reading. If this scope difference were somehow predictable from the presence of the DISTRIBUTED component, then this component would affect truth-value. The scope difference shows up even when the *every* is not in the Subject:

(17)   A boy kissed all the girls.
(18)   A boy kissed every girl/each girl.

There are two situations involved, diagrammed as (c) and (d):

The (c) reading can be represented:

> (c) There is a boy that for all (each of) the girls kissed them (her).
> $\exists y \, \forall x$ (same)

The (d) reading:

> (d) For all (each of) the girls there is a boy who kissed them (her).
> $\forall x \, \exists y$ (same)

Now (17) strongly prefers the (c) situation, but (18) can have either reading. Apparently the tendency of *every* to take wide scope allows it to get to the left of the existential quantifier even though it follows it in the sentence— *all* is not "strong enough" to overcome the handicap.

   Much work has been done on quantifier scope in the attempt to give the rules relating logical representations to sentences. One of the first discoveries was that the facts are subject to considerable dialectal variation: my intuitions are none too certain, and I expect others to disagree with some of them. It seems fairly clear why this is so: these sentences, and the need to discriminate their readings, do not turn up very often—conceivably misunderstanding could occur and go unrecognized, and hence the rule one was applying would go uncorrected. If quantifier intuitions affect the reader as they do me, (s)he is strongly advised to get a cup of coffee or some Gatorade at this point, for we are not quite finished.

   Returning to sentences lacking explicit quantifiers, but this time not generic, consider what is meant by (19) and (20):

(19)   The boys saw the girls.
(20)   The boys kissed the girls.

For the first, the general sense is that all saw all, which has a logical representation of

(19′) $\forall x \, \forall y \, ((\text{BOY}(x) \ \& \ \text{GIRL}(y)) \rightarrow (\text{SEE}(x, y)))$

which could be translated 'For each boy and each girl, he saw her'. This is not unnatural. But (20) does not necessarily claim that each boy kissed each girl, only that the girls got kissed and the boys did it. The logical form parallel to (19′) would be too strong. We might consider the "weaker" formulation:

(20′) $\forall x \, \exists y \, ((\text{BOY}(x) \, \& \, \text{GIRL}(y)) \rightarrow (\text{KISS}(x, y)))$
   For each boy there was a girl he kissed

but this formulation fails to capture the fact that most of the girls got kissed: the formula is compatible with a situation where only one girl got kissed by the boys. Bierwisch (1971: 415–16) argues on the basis of these facts that a proper logic for natural language must allow quantifiers to operate over sets of individuals, not just individuals as in standard quantificational logic. McCawley (1968: 154) suggests using a new quantifier, which he calls the "set-exhaustion quantifier." In any case, standard quantificational logic does not provide any natural way to represent the way sentences like (20) are understood.

One more major difference of logic and language has to do with what is called "jointness," which appears as the source of three extra readings for (21):

(21)   The boys slept with the girls.

Here we have five distinguishable situations, the last three of which are the "group sex" situations:

   (a) Each boy slept with each girl.
   (b) Each boy and each girl had a partner. } as before
   (c) The boys together slept with each girl.
   (d) The boys together slept with the girls together.
   (e) The boys each slept with the girls together.

(Jointness seems the opposite of Jackendoff's *multiple*—1972: 305ff.) Note that the joint reading is incompatible with the DISTRIBUTED component —hence *each* and *every* can be used to eliminate the joint readings:

(22)   Every boy slept with every girl.

Here again we see that plural noun phrases cannot be interpreted simply as a collection of individuals. Logicians are inventive people, however, and new notations are being devised. Quine's claim of some twenty-five years ago (cited in Vendler, 1967: 71) that "Quantification cuts across the vernacular use of 'all', 'every', 'any', and also 'some', 'a certain', etc. , . . . in such a fashion as to clear away the baffling tangle of ambiguities and obscurities" seems to have been premature.

·6.3

Connectives

and/but/although

Most elementary logic books state that the symbol '&' ('·' is equally common or more so) is pretty adequately translated by *and* as long as we are talking about connecting sentences (and not phrases), but they usually tell you soon afterward that it also is translated by *but* and *although*. This amounts to the claim that (23) through (25) are logically (i.e., truth-functionally) equivalent.

(23) John went to bed early and washed the dishes in the morning.
(24) John went to bed early but washed the dishes in the morning.
(25) Although John went to bed early, he washed the dishes in the morning.

Here we have a classic case where logical equivalence falls short of what most people would call sameness of meaning. Obviously one would have a different view of things if he heard (24) or (25) on the one hand, or (23) on the other. The problem is how to capture this difference. Usually it is said to involve some element of contrastiveness with *but* and some element of concession with *although* absent with *and*. But these elements cannot be definitional components, or they would affect the truth-value of the connectives—the connectives then would not be logically equivalent. Here again the term *presupposition* has been invoked, but it is possible to argue that the element of contrast is attached to the term *but* and it is up to the hearer to figure out what the basis of contrast is, or what the Speaker thinks it is, or thinks *he* thinks it is, or is generally thought to be. A second matter often mentioned as a property of *and, but*, and *although* is that there must be some relation or common topic between the sentences so joined, howsoever remote that may be. Kempson (1975) argues, however, that this notion is simply the constraint on connected discourse as such, not a property of the connectives per se. (So also Wilson, 1975: 96f.)

While I believe that these positions are correct—the connectives themselves are very open with regard to the particular connections—what remains to be studied and explained is on what basis speakers, lacking the usual contextual information, manage to arrive at the same inferred connections. Thus I would suppose most people would interpret the *but* in (2) in terms of some such inference as 'going to bed early indicates a desire to put off doing the dishes indefinitely'—hence *but* . . . . The conclusion that this is not a semantic matter does not make it less interesting psychologically. Robin Lakoff (1971) has some interesting observations.

or/unless

We have already noted that logicians define two senses of English *or* and sometimes symbolize them as 'V' (inclusive or conjunctive) and '∧' (exclusive or disjunctive) *or*. Quirk et al. (1972: 563) observe that *or* usually is interpreted exclusively, especially when it is accompanied by *either*:

> Either we operate or the patient will die.

but one can add 'or both', which shows that the exclusive interpretation is not forced even with *either*. Referential and pragmatic considerations can enter in to suppress the inclusive reading:

> John will win or Harry will.

Since we assume there will be only one winner, the inclusive sense is ruled out. *Or*-sentences that amount to conditional threats share the property of *if*-threats of strongly suggesting the exclusive reading:

> You must eat all your dinner or you will get no dessert.
> If you don't eat your dinner, you won't get any dessert.

Apparently the pressure toward exclusive *or* depends on the Speaker's being assumed able to guarantee the outcome—hence,

> Study hard or you won't get into medical school.

can have the inclusive reading ("Who says I will if I do?").

Like *or, unless* is usually exclusively interpreted:

> Unless you eat your dinner, you will get no dessert.

but it can also be inclusive:

> He'll die unless we operate (though he may even if we do).

There is a special limitation to *unless* described by Michael Geis (1973: 235) that the circumstance expressed by the *unless* clause is the unique determining factor: under all other circumstances than that you eat your dinner, you will get no dessert. Thus it does not lend itself to a string of *unless* conditions:

> ?Unless you eat your dinner and unless we have ice cream, you will get no dessert.

> ?I won't go swimming unless the water's warm and unless I won't have to wear trunks. (Example from Bolinger, 1975: 239 n.)

I'm not sure these are ungrammatical or contradictory, however, hence it is hard to decide whether *unless* is LOGICALLY different from *or* or not.

if/when/in case/in the event/provided, providing that (and others)

Since the entailment symbol → is usually said to be translated as *if*, it is useful to review its properties. If S_1 entails S_2, then whenever S_1 is true,

S_2 will be true also (but S_2 could be true also when S_1 is false). We can symbolize:

(26) If it is raining outside, the cellar is damp.
       (raining outside) → (cellar damp)

(27) If the cellar is damp, it is raining outside.
       (cellar damp) → (raining outside)

It is not hard to see that these are not logically equivalent: one could have leaky pipes in the cellar and (26) could be true but not (27); on the other hand, a dry cellar in a rainstorm is compatible with the truth of (27) but not (26). Thus far the translation of → as *if* seems quite reasonable.

There is a strong tendency, however, to interpret *if* in some sentences (threats, promises, lawlike statements, commands) in a stronger way quite parallel to exclusive *or*:

(28) If we don't operate, the patient will die.

If *if* is read simply as →, then the situation of operation and dead patient is quite compatible with (28), but (28) would again most likely be taken as guaranteeing the survival of the operated-on patient. This interpretation amounts to taking *if* as expressing mutual entailment, "if and only if" as the logicians say ('↔' as they symbolize). Geis and Zwicky (1971) have called this tendency an "invited inference"—not a proper one, but one that arises when *if* is used in sentences conveying threats, promises, etc. An alternative view is possible, however: the mutual-entailment (or biconditional) reading could be viewed as a separate sense of *if* (parallel to the treatment of *or* above), and the choice between them would be influenced by referential or pragmatic considerations.

If there is a general principle such as that suggested by Geis and Zwicky at work, then one would expect it to work for other items with similar meanings—specifically items that can convey entailment, such as *when* or *in the event that*. Can we read *when* as 'when and only when' in (29), or *in the event that* as 'just in the event that' in (30)?

(29) When the cellar is damp, it is raining.
(30) In the event that we do not operate, the patient will die.

I think I can, though for some murky reason, probably having to do with implicit knowledge of causes of wet cellars, I find it easier to get the 'if and only if' reading for (29) than (31):

(31) When it is raining, the cellar is damp.

What about (32)?

(32) When it is raining in Chicago, it is dry in Phoenix.

Here no "effect . . . cause" rationale seems likely, and I find the 'if and only if' reading harder to get. The pattern suggests that the model advanced for *or* earlier should work here: there are two senses of *if*, with referential and pragmatic considerations suppressing one reading or another.

There iṣ another reason so to conclude. If there is a general principle extending *if* and some other items from a "proper" '→' to an '↔', then we would not expect to find items that are only ↔. But such items do exist: Quirk et al. cite *providing/provided* (*that*):

(33) Providing that we do not operate, the patient will die.
(34) Provided it is raining, the cellar is damp.

Example (33) seems to commit one to 'if and only if' (↔) without ambi-·guity, and (34) seems to assert that rain is the only cause of cellar dampness (in the relevant context). Quirk et al. suggest also *on condition that* and *as long as* having the 'if and only if' sense solely. Interestingly, the dictionaries I have consulted list 'on condition that' as a sense of *if* distinct from 'in the event that'. It seems reasonable to claim that whatever sense-extension principle is involved, the 'if and only if' sense has been semanticized (i.e., established as a separate sense for *if*).

When raises the interesting relation of universal quantifiers to entailment. As noted earlier,

All men are mortal.

is usually symbolized:

$\forall x \ ((MAN(x)) \to (MORTAL(x)))$
For all x, if x is a man, he is mortal

Generic sentences, though the quantifier is less than universal, have also been symbolized with an entailment:

Children cry: 'For the whole set $\dot{x}$, if x is a child, x cries'
Smokers get cancer: 'For the whole set x, if x is a smoker, x gets cancer'

The quantifier with *when(ever)* seems to quantify over events rather than individuals and to assert that whenever there is an event of rain, there is an event of cellar dampness, and so on. Work now being done on quantification over events doubtless will explicate these relationships. In any case, my dictionaries list a separate sense of *when* for sentences such as

(35) The batter is out when he bunts foul with two strikes on him.

which differs from the previous sense in not entailing the existence of any such events (and see Exercise 6). Ballard, Conrad, and Longacre (1971) report that the connective *nem* in Inibaloi (a Philippine language) is very like English *when* in its capacity to express either overlapping time or logical condition, and when used for logical condition, to suggest the likelihood of the condition. There is another connective in Inibaloi (*no*) which, like *if* in English, does not suggest the likelihood of the condition.

cause

Though not a connective in the logical sense, *cause* is germane because a number of people have attempted to render its sense in terms of an entailment connective. David Dowty (1972: 125) asserts that (36) and (37) are logically equivalent:

(36) If John hadn't put the lampshade on his head, Mary wouldn't have left the party.

(37) John's putting the lampshade on his head caused Mary to leave the party.

Problems with this analysis, however, are raised by Barbara Abbott (1974). Basically, the problem is picking out the relevant necessary conditions to explain what is weird about (39) in terms of what is weird about (38), which seems logically impeccable:

(38) If John hadn't been born, he wouldn't have gotten married.

(39) John's being born caused him to get married.

In a recent text in elementary logic, Benson Mates (1972) states the logic teacher's quandary: "The task of translating the natural language into our artificial language is still one for which it is practically impossible to find systematic rules" (69). He advises the student to adopt a procedure that works better than there is any reason to believe it should: "To translate a sentence of the natural language into the artificial language $\mathfrak{L}$, ask yourself what the natural language sentence means, and then try to find a sentence of $\mathfrak{L}$ which, relative to a standard specification of an interpretation, has as nearly as possible that same meaning" (69–70). What Mates appears to mean by *meaning* is not conceptual structure but states of affairs that the sentence would be true of (i.e., the situations represented by diagrams here). The practical aid to translation then involves reference to the world:

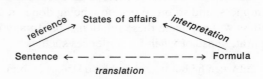

One translates by determining that the sentence and formulas refer to the same state of affairs. This replaces one mystery with another, since we have not specified how we determine the states of affairs that sentences refer to. If we had an explicit set of translation rules, then we would need only one specification of reference, namely from formula to world. We can, for example, stipulate a reference protocol (Mates' "specification of an interpretation") for formulas with quantifiers: when the existential quantifier stands outside the universal, a single, specific individual is to be sought, but when the ∃ is inside the ∀, the entailment is only of the existence of *some* individual (i.e., the *same* individual need not be involved). This is what we have done in 15(a) and (b), for example. Then, if we specify the translation of sentence and formula, we provide an explicit account of the meaning of the sentence. Such a theory would be able to predict "referential" cancellation of logically possible readings. The predicate *win*, for example, could have linked to it the notation (however it is to be formalized) that for a given event, there is only one x such that x wins, so that the inclusive *or* sense (V) is cancelled for

John will win or Harry will.

There remains the need for a pragmatic theory that will account for how sentences are understood in actual situations: how information given in the situation specifies reference, suppresses logically possible readings, and adjusts or shifts "literal" senses to give rise to conversational implicatures. The next chapter will discuss some work that has been done in the direction of defining and formulating pragmatics.

READINGS FOR CHAPTER VI

The bibliography for these topics is immense and very little of it introductory. There is a bibliography by Partee, Sabsay, and Soper (1971).

The treatment of *all* and *every* is partly taken from Reichenbach (1947), which is frequently taken as a starting point in recent discussions.

G. Lakoff (1970) has an early (1965) discussion of quantifiers, negation, and scope as an appendix. This was very influential in introducing the topics into linguistics.

Carden (1974: esp. Section 8) discusses quantifier dialects as they bear on various formalizations.

Lawler (1972 and 1973) discusses problems in symbolizing generics. But see also Nunberg and Pan (1975).

Scope relations with quantifiers and negatives are discussed at much greater length in Kroch (1975). He notes, for example, several factors that induce a preference for one scope reading over another and shows that a claim that *every* always has wide scope would be wrong:

A woman (with a mole on her right cheek) won the vote of every judge.

The extra descriptive material induces a wide-scope preference for the existential —i.e., suggests that a single individual is being described. Kroch attempts to give the translation rules.

For a general discussion of pragmatic considerations selecting "preferred readings," see Wilson (1975: Chapter 5).

EXERCISES AND PROBLEMS

1. How many readings can you get for
   The three hunters shot two deer.

   Which ones for
   Two deer were shot by the three hunters.

2. Can you explain the oddity of (b)?
   (a)　Every man has a mother.
   (b)　?All men have a mother.

3. Are the following logically equivalent? If not, why not?
   (a)　The target wasn't hit by many arrows.
   (b)　Many arrows didn't hit the target.

4. Is *because* more like *cause*, or more like *if*? Consider:
   If it is raining in Chicago, it will be here in a few hours.
   Because it is raining in Chicago, it will be here in a few hours.
   Rain in Chicago causes rain here a few hours later.

5. Explain what *though* is doing in the following (cf. *and*):
   He'll die if we don't operate, though he may if we do.

6. Why can't one get the 'if and only if' sense for *when* in (35)?

7. Must generics be added to the list of environments where a noun phrase does not entail the existence of a referent? Cf.:
   A gentleman opens doors for ladies.

VII

Pragmatics

The previous chapters have assumed that it is reasonable to talk about the meanings of words, phrases, and sentences without regard to the contexts in which they are used. Linguists working under this assumption have in recent years come to realize its limits: not all the aspects of meaning are describable without reference to context, some meanings change in certain contexts, and some conditions on sensible (nonanomalous) statements seem to involve beliefs shared by Speaker and Hearer about the things referred to, or general factual probabilities. The term *pragmatics* is now used to refer to the systematic interaction of sentences with contexts. It is also used to refer to judgments that involve factual assumptions, though in the following sections I will use the term more narrowly to refer to nongeneral knowledge and beliefs involved in situations of use.

The classic examples of dependence on context are definiteness and deixis. When a Speaker uses the definite article with a nominal, he assumes that the referent of the nominal is known to, or in the mind of, the Hearer. Hence if one walks into a classroom and says, "The midterm will be on Wednesday," when no previous mention has been made of any tests, the

Hearers are entitled to be a little taken aback (shall we say?). This is true also for personal pronouns: if you initiate a conversation with "He left for New York at 10," your Hearer may wonder why you assume that the referent of *he* is in his mind (cf. *Waiting for Godot*). Deictic terms include tense, the demonstrative articles and pronouns (*this, that*), and such pro-adverbs as *here, there*. All of these require a situation known both to Speaker and Hearer to be interpreted. A sentence like

> I was here just this morning.

is singularly uninformative unless we know who is speaking (or writing), when, and where. Once these things are established in discourse, the definite article and definite pronominal forms can be used. In speech, of course, time, place, and speaker are evident. Section 7.1 will take up the deictic words in more detail.

Sometimes what must be established in a discourse is not a referent but a relationship between things. The oddities in Problem 2 of Chapter II:

> He was so rich he snored.
> He was too drunk to get chickenpox.
> He was not intelligent enough to paint his bathroom purple.

appear to be odd because they assume some causal connection between having the property and the behavior indicated, although *causal* is perhaps too strong a term:

> If one is rich, one tends to snore.
> The richer one is, the more he tends to snore.
> Richness causes snoring.

There is a lot more to this, but the general point is clear enough: the general condition involves a belief about factual relations between properties and their consequences rather than anything inherent in the meanings of the words. Similarly with purpose expressions: Chisato Kitagawa (1974) points out that a general constraint is that the Speaker or doer believe the action he performs can effect the result he desires:

> She wore a red dress to pass the bar examination.

leads one to suspect that at least in her mind the bar examiners are susceptible to forces that most of us assume they are not.

The "connection" between things need not always be causal. Steven Smith (1972) has noted that there is something odd about the first pair of sentences in contrast to the second:

> ?Rita Sue is only stupid, she isn't pretty.
> ?Rita Sue is stupid, but she isn't pretty.
> Rita Sue is only stupid, she isn't ugly.
> Rita Sue is stupid, but she isn't ugly.

Smith suggests that here both properties must be either desirable or undesirable. It seems to me, however, that all that is necessary to render the first two plausible is a situation in which one is discussing the general correlation of intelligence and good looks, where Rita Sue is cited as a counter-example to the generalization 'If a girl is stupid, she's sure to be pretty'. In other words, Smith's desirable/undesirable notion is only one way to account for a pairing of traits—speakers might establish their own pairings for the purposes of discussion. The "common topic" constraint of coordinate conjunction is of like nature. The following seems odd:

Simon was elected and/but two dogs are fighting outside.

only because it is a little hard, out of context, to imagine what connection exists in the Speaker's mind. One can imagine possible connections, but the actual or most likely one in a given instance cannot be determined from the form or meaning of the sentence. Other shared assumptions of Speaker and Hearer will be discussed in Section 7.2.

A third aspect of pragmatics concerns certain general assumptions Speaker and Hearer are entitled to make about each other's probable behavior and feelings that may lead them into various "indirections" as they engage in various speech acts. The general principles will be sketched in Section 7.3 in regard to the acts of Requesting and Offering.

29.3.82   **7.1**

Deixis

As is obvious and well known, tense or time deixis is assigned relative to a 'now" of utterance, with simple past tense locating an event or state of affairs "before now," though (as John Anderson, 1973, notes) it may reflect the pastness of the existence of the referent of the subject:

The dodo was a bird.

That is, the classification of dodos as birds is "past" because dodos are "past."

The present perfect tense in English also locates an event or state of affairs in the past, but conveys the extra notion that the event/state has some relevance for the present. Hence its sense is often given as 'by or until now'. In the case of inchoative or causative verbs, the most likely interpretation would be that the result of the change continues into the present, but with other verbs the present relevance is less determinate:

Hilary has climbed Mt. Everest.
The lake has frozen.

Even in the latter (inchoative) sentence, duration-of-result is not necessarily meant (i.e., entailed), since it could be a reply to a claim that the lake has never frozen. One kind of present relevance is what McCawley (1971) calls "hot news"—any past event that is presumed by the Speaker to be news to the Hearer may be cast in the present perfect: *Nixon has resigned.* "Hot news" doesn't remain hot for long, usually, but the same sentence could be used at a later date if, say, the Speaker were reviewing all of the bizarre events that had occurred since President Kennedy's assassination. Present perfects are uncomfortable when the Subject is "past" (*Einstein has visited Princeton*—noted by Chomsky, 1971, and others), but this probably is a reflection of the general assumption of present existence associated with Subjects rather than a peculiarity of perfects as such. Throughout this book I have used the present perfect to describe ideas put forth by writers in publications that have appeared in the last few decades, assuming that the ideas have "current relevance" for the discussion—a past tense gives rise to the assumption that the ideas are no longer currently entertained, perhaps because proven false.

The devices for locating things in space relative to Speaker and Hearer are more complicated than those for time, because while Speaker and Hearer are assumed to be at the same point in time, they are not necessarily so in place. The *here/there, this/that* oppositions appear to be like time at first glance if we think of Speaker (S) and Hearer (H) as together:

> **S**
>
>   *A*   *B*
>
> **H**

Both Speaker and Hearer would refer to *A* as *this one (here)* and *B* as *that one (there)*. The system gets more complicated, however, when *A* and *B* lie between S and H:

>   *B*
>
> **S**   **H**
>
>   *A*

Then for Speaker, *A* is *here, B there*, but vice versa for Hearer. For Hearer to understand which thing Speaker is referring to by *this one*, Hearer must adopt Speaker's point of view, as it were, for the moment. Clark and Sengul (1974) have reported that children do not at first switch points of view, but always make assignments from their point of view, and may go through two transitional stages where they take the Speaker's point of view for *there/that* but not *this/here* or vice versa, before arriving at the adult ability to switch for all relevant instances. This is quite parallel to Piaget's (1959: 108) findings about *right* and *left*.

Roughly the same elements are marked with the verbs *come* and *go*, *bring* and *take*, though there is a complicating factor in the Speaker's ability to imagine that either or both are not where they literally are but where they were or will be. Ignoring this complication for a moment, we as speakers can specify that in the following situation:

                                    B   C

either *B* or *C* could say to the other *go into the house*, but *A* would be addressing *B* or *C* or both in *come into the house*, and similarly if there were a plate with *B* and *C*, either *B* or *C* could say *take the plate into the house* to the other, but *A* would say *bring the plate into the house*. The complication arises in the possibility of *B* or *C* adopting the "in-house" point of view: if, e.g., *B* is going into the house, *B* can say *come into the house (and bring the plate)* to *C*. This also occurs when we, at home, say:

He didn't come to work today.

if we were at work earlier. Basically, however, the Speaker of *come/bring* is assumed to be at the Goal of the motion, and the Speaker of *go/take* not at the Goal.

Clark and Garnica (1974) have shown that children at first appear not to distinguish the two members of these pairs, analyzing them both with Speaker at the Goal. This gives the appearance of understanding *come/bring* but not *go/take*, though in fact their sense of *come* is incompletely specified. Data from this study also give the impression that even younger children do reverse perspectives, since they will identify *A* as the Hearer of a question, "Can I come into the house?" which if said by *B* or *C* to himself would be, "I wonder if I can go into the house?" Clark and Garnica show, however, that this impression is mistaken, since the children will also identify *A* as the Hearer of "Can I go into the house?"—in short, the one at the Goal is always assumed to be the Hearer of questions as well as the Speaker of commands. Only later, and after trying alternative strategies, do they master the assignment of Speaker and Hearer coded by adults.

In an interesting by-product of her work on the acquisition of these terms, Clark (1974) showed that the notions of "hereness" associated with *come* and "thereness" with *go* carry over to idiomatic extensions of *come* and *go*. Hereness is extended to mean "normal state," which includes such things as consciousness, emotional equilibrium, and other good things:

He came to./He went under.
He came back to earth./He went beserk.
He came of age./He went bald at thirty.

though conceivably the last might be ok with *come* in a Bald is Beautiful group. One slightly darker note:

It came undone/unraveled/apart.

where the "normal" state, alas, appears to be that of disorder.

The familiarity of the *this/that, come/go* division may obscure the fact that deictic distinctions need not be packed into a two-term opposition. Spanish and Japanese (Kuno, 1973), for example, make three-way distinctions among proforms such as

Japanese
$$\left\{\begin{array}{l} \textit{kore} - \text{'the one near the Speaker'} - \textit{esto} \\ \textit{sore} - \text{'the one near the Hearer'} \quad - \textit{eso} \\ \textit{are} \; - \text{'the one away from both'} \quad - \textit{aquello} \end{array}\right\} \text{Spanish}$$

Obviously this system presents the child learning Japanese or Spanish with a slightly different set of problems. One might suppose that the child would generalize *sore* and *are* and use *are* at first, since the "reversal of perspective" involved in using *sore* does not come easy, at least to Western children. This prediction could be tested, and the relative order of emergence would be an interesting check on the putative universality of the strategies that appear in the experiments with English.

In "May We Come In?" Charles Fillmore (1973a) points out that the various pragmatic aspects of a sentence may work together to eliminate potential ambiguities much as selectional features do. The modal auxiliary *may* has at least two senses, one having to do with permission (the "root" or "deontic" sense), the other with possibility (the "epistemic" sense). *We* can be taken as including the Hearer (Shall we get together later?—inclusive *we*) or not (We are waiting for you to tell us what to do—exclusive *we*). The sentence *May we come in?*, however, is not four ways ambiguous. The epistemic sense of *may* is cancelled by its use in a question (*May it rain?* is not possible unless addressed to the weather-god.) Fillmore argues that permission-seeking plus *come* cancel the inclusive *we* sense: the Hearer is understood not to be included in the *we*. This follows from two lines of attack: usually the ones seeking permission are distinct from the one(s) granting it, and second, given *come*, someone has to be at the destination, permission to go to which is being sought. Since the Speaker and associate(s) are not at the reference point of *come* (the Speaker is adopting the Hearer's point of view), the Speaker and Hearer are at different points and do not cohere spatially as a group. The Hearer therefore is not included, is understood to be at the reference point, and is understood to be a permission grantor (i.e., to have the authority to grant or withhold permission for Speaker and associate(s) to come to the place where Speaker is).

Old/New Information

In discussions of speech acts (which will be taken up in the following section) the speech act of asserting or Informing someone of something is
said to have a preparatory or setting condition: the Speaker assumes the
Hearer does not already know the information, though presumably would
want to or should know it. Usually, not all of the information in a sentence
spoken by the Speaker in Informing is "new" to the Hearer—typically the
new part is put toward the end of the sentence and in speech receives the
accent (other terms are: peak of the intonation contour, nucleus of the tone
group, main sentential stress). If more than one item is new, usually the
item that in the Speaker's estimation is the most significant piece of new
information receives the accent, or at least the primary accent ('). This item
is sometimes called the **focus** of the sentence. The distribution of accent
according to these considerations can be seen in pairings of sentences with
questions that represent the "presupposed" or "known" information. The
following are not to be taken as actual question-answer sequences, which
would pronominalize or delete parts of the answer:

(1)   Who killed the duck?   Jóhn killed the duck.

(2)   What did John do to the duck? John kílled the duck.

(3) a. Which bird did John kill?
    b. What did John kill?   John killed the dúck.
    c. What did John do?

The syntactic constructions of Clefts (4 and 6) and Pseudoclefts (5 and 7)
can be used to highlight the focus:

(4)   It was Jóhn who killed the duck.

(5)   What John did to the duck was (to) kíll it.

(6)   It was the dúck that John killed.

(7)   What John did was kill the dúck.

Note that (6) and (7) separate two possible interpretations of *John killed the
dúck*: where *the duck* is focused, we get (6), where *kill the duck* is the
focus, we get (7). Matters get complicated very quickly, however. For one
thing, what is new may be a pairing of items rather than the identification
of them, as would be the answer to:

> I noticed Bob and Ted and Carol and Alice all at the party. Who was
> with whom?

For another, as (3a) shows, the new information may be only some of the components of the focused word. In general, the focused item can be said to contrast with a relevant class of possible alternatives in the situation, but it is not possible to specify exactly what those alternatives are from the sentence out of context.

The words *even, only,* and *just* introduce the notion of "contrast to expectation" in a more pointed way:

(8)   Even John has killed a duck.

(9)   Only John has killed a duck.

What *even* adds in (8) is the notion that John was the least likely one to commit an act of duck-slaughter. (8) appears to assume also that others have done so. What *only* adds in (9) is that others did not commit duck-slaughter, though the assumption is conveyed that they might have. Clearly (10) and (11) do not mean precisely the same things that (8) and (9) do:

(10) a. John has even kílled a duck.

        b. John has even killed a dúck.

(11) a. John has only kílled a duck.

        b. John has only killed a dúck.

In (10) it is either the act of killing (= a) or its being done to ducks (= b) that is considered unlikely and assumed to be done by others, not John's having committed it. In (11) the contrast is similarly to either other more extreme things done to ducks (a) or other, more important, beasts than ducks (b), and the assumption is that he was expected to have done greater things. One can see that the "scope" of these words varies in a regular way with their position and the focus chosen. There are a number of interesting attempts to formulate the rules pairing readings with positions in the sentence and placements of accent. (See Jackendoff, 1972; S. Anderson, 1972; Fraser, 1971; Horn, 1969.)

The paraphrases of (11) raise a further pragmatic point about *only*—namely, that it conveys the notion of falling short of more extreme expectations, though presumably such scaling of extremity is done more or less ad hoc in a given conversation. The contrasts to *kill* in (11a), for example, would go in one direction in a conversation about becoming a butcher and another in a conversation about sadistic and unnatural things people might do to ducks. Laurence Horn (1969) notes that

Muriel only voted for Hubert, she didn't do the laundry.

is a little odd out of context because of the difficulty of getting the two items on some "scale of degree of strength," as Horn calls it. We may imagine some possibilities, however—e.g., a discussion of the subservient role a politician's wife is expected to play in our society. Nonetheless, the notion of "scales of degree of strength" seems right as a tendency and apparently extends to *even* as well, since (8) suggests 'no less ( ) than John' and (10b) 'no less a ( ) than a duck', where the blanks must be filled in with information from context (e.g., no less a pacifist than John, no less difficult a target than a duck, not just ants and flies but a duck).

Suppose the Speaker is not sure whether what he proposes to tell the Hearer is in fact new to the Hearer. Uninformative statements are common enough and have various functions (*It's cold this morning!*), but to inform someone of something he already knows is socially awkward, since informing him shows that you think he is "out of it," that your information is superior to his. One way to avoid such awkwardness is to ask him if he knows:

> Did you know that your left rear tire is nearly flat?

This is fairly polite, though it forces him to say "Yes" or "No." It would be even more polite to say:

> I just noticed that your left rear tire is nearly flat.

where he can claim knowledge superior to yours if he wishes, agree that that sort of thing can happen unnoticed, etc. Although a general maxim of informing people of things is that we tell them the most that we know (noted in Chapter I), considerations of politeness may induce us to soften indications of certainty:

> I think they stay open until 10 on Saturdays.
> I believe you make it with bourbon.
> I have a hunch you won't find it.

where the Speaker may be certain of the facts but unwilling to insist on his certainty. Why *think* and *believe,* which literally affirm a precondition of informing, function as softeners here is a little mysterious. When accented, however, they have a sense contrasting with *I am súre that . . .* , which may carry over even to the unstressed form. It is a very general pattern, however, for affirming or questioning a precondition of a speech act to indirectly convey the speech act.

The discussion of the notions of old and new information was simplified by the assumption of mention in immediately prior discourse (the "question-and-answer" paradigm). In real conversations, the Speaker treats as old information things that are situationally present to him and the Hearer and things implicit in conversation. Chafe (1974) notes that considerable delicacy is required in the assessment of what is established in the Hearer's consciousness, and we all know children and other people who assume that the connections they make are automatically made by their Hearers. Long after children learn that their Hearers do not in every case see what they see, they will continue to assume that their Hearers associate things as they do and remember what they have experienced. We judge adults who indulge in this as preoccupied, self-absorbed, rude, or in radical cases as schizophrenic, but in children this egocentricity is softened by their ignorance that others are unlikely to share their associations.

Children of age 3 or 4 often alarm or disconcert their parents with out-of-the-blue statements like *That boy hurt me*, which, on questioning, refer to an event of a week before. Chafe (1973) observes that in adult speech such an event would normally be mentioned with a time adverbial (e.g., *last week*), since the event is no longer likely to be in the "surface memory" of the Hearer—i.e., the Hearer cannot be expected to be immediately conscious of the time at which the event occurred. (Chafe also notes the relation of this to the "present relevance" of present perfect tense.) Chafe notes, however, that the span of time an event remains in surface memory varies with its importance to the Speaker. One explanation for the child's sentence is that the hurting-event was sufficiently significant to overcome the time lag. Another explanation is that Chafe's distinction of modes of memory into surface, shallow, and deep is less developed in the child, or at least that the conventional marking of the levels has not been learned. In any case, there is a lack of awareness of what is likely to be remembered, and in what way, in the Hearer's mind. Research on the question of the conventional aspects of the introduction and connection of ideas in discourse might yield some insight into what we mean by certain types of mental illness.

7.3

Strategies of Indirection

There are a number of approaches to speech acts, differing with regard to how many there are, how they should be classified, and how the ability speakers have to perform them should be formalized. The Readings give a number of the main approaches. The starting point for recent work is the work of the Oxford philosopher John L. Austin, who called attention to the fact that a great deal of language is not simple assertion in a vacuum but is involved with performing actions and hence in getting people to do things. Verbs and constructions, the saying of which performs a speech act and says it is performed, have come to be called **performatives.** These include the italicized verbs in

I *tell* you that it is broken.

> I *request* of you that you tell me where the bathroom is.
> I *order* you to stop banging the door.

One can classify performative verbs according to the type of speech act they perform, where the type of act is usually called by one of the verbs of the group—e.g., Requesting, Informing, etc.—and these general speech acts are sometimes called **illocutionary** acts. Since one may perform the acts without actually using a performative verb, the things he says are said to have the "illocutionary force" of one of the appropriate performative verbs. Treating questions as Requests, one may say that

> Where is the bathroom?

has the illocutionary force of a Request, as does the following spoken with rising intonation:

> The bathroom is upstairs

Most languages have special forms to carry out the illocutionary acts of Requesting and Ordering (if these should be distinguished: many writers treat one as a subtype of the other). There are also ways in which sentences that are declarative in form can function as (i.e., have the force of) a Request or Order, and interrogatives can function as Requests for something other than what they literally request. What is particularly interesting is that they undergo these shifts in illocutionary force in a quite regular way, and hence there are rules that speakers somehow learn. I will illustrate these rules in regard to Requests and Offers (which are the flip side of Requests), basing the account primarily on Gordon and Lakoff (1971), but with some influence from Robin Lakoff (1972), Bruce Fraser (1974a, b), and Bernard Mohan (1974).

To Request the Hearer to do something (call it P) in good faith ("sincerely") the Speaker must

(A) want the Hearer to do P

and must assume certain things (preparatory conditions[1]) about the Hearer:

(B) think that the Hearer is able to do P;
(C) think that the Hearer is not unwilling to do P;
(D) think that the Hearer does not intend to do P, and hence will not do P, unless asked.

Sentences that simultaneously request and deny one of these conditions are "pragmatically contradictory":

[1]These are sometimes called felicity conditions and sometimes divided into "sincerity" conditions and "preparatory" or "setting" conditions.

(A′) Please take out the garbage, even though I don't want you to.
(B′) Please take out the garbage, even if you can't.
(C′) Please take out the garbage, although I know you adamantly refuse to.
(D′) Please take out the garbage, although you're obviously going to anyway.
       way.

Instead of a flat Request, the Speaker can say:

(1)   I want you to take out the garbage.

which literally informs the Hearer that condition A of a Request is the case. From this, the Hearer can infer the Request itself according to a general principle:

> *Expression of Desire*: Given nothing to suggest to the contrary, whenever a Speaker expresses his desire for some state of affairs to come about, one can infer that he is seeking (Requesting) the Hearer's cooperation in bringing about this state of affairs.
>
> —Modified from Fraser, 1974b: 17

'Cooperation' may range from the permission of the Hearer:

> I want to tell you something.

through the Hearer's refraining from interfering:

> I want to go to sleep.

to the Hearer's active participation:

> I want to play gin rummy.

or to the Hearer's performing the action, as in the example at hand (1). The Principle of Expression of Desire, then, enables the Hearer to infer that the Speaker's purpose in saying (1) is not to inform the Hearer of the Speaker's desires but to Request his cooperation. Since Requests are understood to be, if unspecified, for performance at the earliest relevant opportunity, Hearer is being uncooperative if he replies to

> "Remind me to take out the garbage."   "OK, take out the garbage."

or, on the other hand, if he waits a week or so to do it. Obviously, when the earliest relevant opportunity is determined by the particular action and situation.

Alternatively, a Speaker might say:

(2)   Can you take out the garbage?

which literally Requests information about whether condition B for a Request is the case. Hearer tries to respond to what he concludes Speaker's purpose is in uttering (2). Hearer knows that Speaker must assume him able to perform the action in order to request him to perform it, so he may infer that Speaker is asking about his ability in order to be in a position to Request. He may, then, if he chooses, respond to (2) as the Request itself, especially if he obviously has the ability. (2) and (1) are softened Requests in that they allow the Hearer the option of not making the inference, or refusing to perform the action without actually refusing a Request (see suggestions for saving face, below).

The other preparatory conditions or preconditions for Requesting also yield indirect Requests. Consider first (3):

(3)   Are you willing to take out the garbage?

Here again the Hearer may apply the same strategy: he may infer that the Speaker wants the literally requested information in order to be in a position to Request the action (assuming, of course, a positive response—Speaker can retreat from the Request if he receives a negative response). Note also that positive responses to (2) and (3) can convey Offers (see below). The last precondition (D) yields such indirect Requests as

(4)   Are you planning to take out the garbage today?
       Do you intend to take out the garbage today?
       Are you going to take out the garbage today?

Again the Hearer knows that a *no* answer will satisfy a condition for a Request and so, if his answer is *no*, he will take (4) as Requests—albeit fairly oblique ones, perhaps having more the force of Suggestions—and reply "OK" instead of *yes* or *no* (note that *yes* amounts to a Promise!). A curious fact in relation to this analysis, however, is that *will* in

(5)   Will you take out the garbage?

is a very direct Request word—that is, (5) is almost impossible to interpret in the question sense that can be given to (4). Here, then, *will* is plainly not equivalent to *be going to* (i.e., is not a simple expression of Future time). Hence (5) is not an indirect or "softened" Request. I do not see how to account for the fact that it does not convey a softened Request along the lines of (1) through (4).

An Offer is a kind of anticipated Request. The Speaker volunteers information necessary for the Hearer to make a Request. When a Speaker Offers to do something (Q), the following conditions obtain:

(E) Speaker wants Hearer's permission to do Q;
     (*Principle of Permission Seeking*: If someone seeks another's permission to do something, we may infer that he wants to do it.)
(F) Speaker believes he is able to do Q;

(G) Speaker is willing to do Q;

(H) Speaker assumes Hearer is not unwilling to permit Speaker to do Q.

If Speaker simultaneously makes an Offer and denies one of the above, he commits pragmatic contradictions again:

(E′) I offer to do the dishes and will do them whatever you say.

(F′) I offer to do the dishes even though I can't.

(G′) I offer to do the dishes though I'd rather die than do them.

(H′) I offer to do the dishes, though I know you won't let me.

The following then should have the potential of conveying Offers:

(6)   I want you to let me do the dishes.

(7)   I can do the dishes.

(8)   I'm willing to do the dishes.

(9)   Will you let me do the dishes?

An interesting variation is the use of a formally imperative sentence:

(10)   Let me do the dishes.

which, like (9), conveys a Request for Permission and hence an Offer via E.

Note that (7) and (8) can also be answers to indirectly conveyed Requests (= 2 and 3). One cannot make an Offer in response to a direct Request, but apparently an indirect Request does allow the Hearer the option of appearing to make an Offer—that is one of the reasons an indirectly conveyed Request is more polite than a direct one. However, an "Offer" in response to a Request must count as a Promise, since there is no doubt in anyone's mind that the Requester will grant the permission.

A speech act may be performed in bad faith. If the Speaker does not actually deny one of the conditions, but in fact does not believe that it holds, then he is not sincerely Offering, Requesting, etc. If, for example, condition G (Speaker is willing) does not hold, the Offer is "pro forma" and "insincere." In extreme cases, where unwillingness is to be presumed, the Offer may be ironic:

> Please let me help you pick my pocket.

Similarly, of course, for Requests: the Request

> Tell me about it.

uttered in a weary voice is likely to get the reply

> Do you really want to know?

which is to say, "Does condition A hold?"—i.e., is the request sincerely made?

Two principles seem to capture fairly well the meaning of politeness in regard to Requests and Offers (and other speech acts as well): Avoid Confrontations and Avoid Exposure. These may be regarded as codifying strategies for protecting the egos of Speaker and Hearer from abrasive or painful conflicts.

AVOID CONFRONTATIONS ("Leave Options"). A direct Request can only be accepted or refused. Both Speaker and Hearer are on the spot, and it may be in Speaker's interest as well as Hearer's to avoid this if possible, leaving Hearer more options in responding. As noted above, indirect Requests can be given literal answers, thus signalling to Speaker whether the Request itself would be "safe" to make. If the answer to an indirect Request is negative, Speaker can back off and avoid losing face. Similarly for Offering: the Speaker may lose face if a direct Offer is declined, and the Hearer be placed in a difficult position, so that indirect offers avoid the potential confrontation. (This consideration at times conflicts with the second principle). Children who are learning these conventions often make use of the conditional rather transparently:

> If I asked you, would you tell me?
> If I offered, would you accept?

Notice that there is a slight difference in degree of politeness between (11) and (12), (13) and (14):

(11) Can I help you?
(12) May I help you?

(13) Can I ask you how much that cost?
(14) May I ask you how much that cost?

The modal auxiliaries seem to function with literal meanings: in (11), the question is literally, "Am I able to help you?"—i.e., are the conditions met for my helping you? A variety of negative responses is possible:

> No, you seem to be sold out.
> I'm just browsing (I am unwilling to accept an offer of help).

With (12), however, the options are narrowed down to refusal of permission to help. Even more obviously, (13) allows a variety of responses:

> I'm afraid I don't know—it was a gift.
> I hate talking about money.
> Are you sure you want to know?

where (14) seems to allow only refusal of permission to Request. Hence (12) and (14), by narrowing options, are blunter, less polite than (11) and (13) (see Robin Lakoff, 1972).

AVOID EXPOSURE, the second principle, involves not putting Hearer on the spot by exposing his ignorance, desires, or lack of ability to respond perfectly freely. In regard to Offers, this results in the tactic:

When Offering, Offer as a favor to the self.

There is a scale of politeness in this regard:

> (a) I suppose you want me to take out the garbage.
> (b) Would you like me to take out the garbage?
> (c) I can take out the garbage if you want.
> (d) Let me take out the garbage.
> (e) I want to take out the garbage.

The first is downright rude, since it directly forces the Hearer to expose his desires. Offers (b) and (c) still involve some exposure on the Hearer's part, but he can choose how to do it. Offers (d) and (e) do not require exposure and are in this regard more polite. There is a countertactic involved here, however, involving Face Saving: an Offer should be easy to decline. Offers (d) and (e) are fairly strong, since to decline them one must refuse something the Speaker has asked for, denying him the gratification of his expressed—or in the case of (d)—implicated wish. Offers (b) and (c), therefore, are more polite than they would seem according to the second principle only.

I think considerations of politeness and face-saving provide a natural explanation for the use of these indirect Requests and Offers. It seems that the acquisition of these strategies of indirection would be a long and late process for children. In a study of videotapes of mothers with their two-year-old children, however, Marilyn Shatz (1974) was surprised to find that the children responded as well to

> Can you pass the salt?
> Is there salt on the table?

as they did to direct imperatives, though they more often accompanied their response of the passing the salt with a verbal response to the indirect forms. Shatz claims that this was relatively independent of nonverbal cues. The research is tricky, however, since the situation itself is cue-laden—even "Salt!" should get the response. Here the children's grasp of the devices is open to question, since there is no indication that they realize the precise force of the utterances, or even that some of them are not simply formulaic for them. Evidence of use of the indirect forms by children is needed, though this is very difficult to obtain—one cannot play "games" with children along the lines of research discussed in previous chapters, and the exact relationship of child and interlocutor is crucial. Children do use indirect modes of requesting, however, for a very obvious reason: it may prove more efficient to do so (particularly with parents who respond to indirectness!). One child I have observed (aged three) will say "I like cheese" as a way of angling for some cheese. The *can you* form does not occur, however, though this may reflect the theory of "parental omnipotence," which is not subject even to nonliteral questioning.

There are certain problems with the treatment of indirect speech acts given here. The principles invoked are broad and not based in a coherent theory of human communication and action. They merely account for shifts of force that do occur and do not rule any shifts out or characterize a natural class of shifts. Also, they leave open the question of what tips the Hearer off that a given utterance does not have literal force. (This is similar to the problem of the recognition of metaphor.) Mohan (1974) suggests a general maxim that the Hearer tries to infer the purpose of the Speaker in saying what he does, and if the sentence taken literally has an improbable purpose, the Hearer is led to consider what indirect act the Speaker means to convey, the purpose of which would be probable. If a stranger walks up to us on the street and says:

Can you tell me where the dog pound is?

we are perhaps unlikely to assume he is doing a survey of citizen awareness of municipal facilities. Obviously this effect will be strengthened if he is dragging a snarling, mangy cur behind him and weakened if he appears to be a sociologist. But obviously in numerous cases one will not be sure whether indirect strategies are involved or not. Sag and Liberman (1975) show, by the way, that intonation can insist on a literal reading in some cases, or suggest an indirect one.

Sadock (1974) suggests that the treatment here, which is essentially like that of a metaphor given earlier, may not be the proper one for all indirect acts: there may be constructions that have developed separate senses because of frequent use parallel to the "figurative" senses some words have developed (and, as argued earlier, some connectives may have developed). He suggests, for example, that *can you* and *will you* may have developed genuine separate imperative senses, while *are you able to* and *are you going to* have not, and do undergo the sorts of shifts described here. This seems an attractive way to account for the unexpected directness of *will* noted above. Much more research remains to be done on this and on most of the topics discussed in this chapter, however, before we will have even a good outline of a theory of pragmatics.

READINGS FOR CHAPTER VII

Many of the papers and authors mentioned here, as well as the famous paper by H. Paul Grice, are represented in the Morgan and Cole collection.

Larkin and O'Malley (1973) discuss declarative sentences not used to inform.

The last part of Kempson (1975) is an examination and development of Grice's model of conversation.

In various publications Susumo Kuno (e.g., 1975) proposes certain refinements on the notion of given or old information and examines constraints on pronominalization and deletion (also position) of elements. The notion of given information is similar to the "Pragmatic Universe of Discourse" in Kempson and to "presupposed information" as it is used by Jackendoff (1972) and Chomsky (1971).

EXERCISES AND PROBLEMS

1. Match the sentences to the contexts they may occur in:

    (a) Jóhn doesn't write poems in the bathroom.

    (b) John doesn't wríte poems in the bathroom.

    (c) John doesn't write póems in the bathroom.

    (d) John doesn't write poems in the báthroom.

    (1) . . . , though he does just about every place else.
    (2) . . . , though Harry does.
    (3) —inspiration never visits him there, though he reads them there enough.
    (4) . . . , though he may compose a few letters there now and then.

2. What relation must obtain between the verbs in the following:

    John called Mary a virgin, and then SHE called HIM a liar.
    John called Mary a virgin, and then SHE insulted HIM.
    John called Mary a virgin, ?and then SHE kissed HIM.
    John called Mary a virgin, ?and then SHE arrested HIM.

3. Usually sentences with *not* are vague with respect to how much of the material following *not* is negated:

    Raskalnikov didn't murder the old woman with a hammer—
        —it was someone else that he murdered
        —he used an ax
        —he executed her
    Does focusing eliminate the vagueness?
                      (´)   (´)   (´)
    Raskalnikov didn't murder the old woman with a hammer.

4. What considerations determine the relative politeness of (a) and (b), assuming the host is speaking?

    (a) Have some more cake.
    (b) Would you like some more cake?

5. How to Warn: All of the following could be spoken with the intent of warning the Hearer (i.e., indirectly convey Warnings). What must the preconditions for Warning be?

   (a) Do you think your daughter will marry that boy she has been dating?
   (b) Do you want your daughter to marry that boy she has been dating?
   (c) I think your daughter will marry that boy she has been dating.
   (d) It's a shame that your daughter is going to marry that boy etc.

6. Rank the preceding in terms of politeness.

7. What sort of inference might a teacher make if a student said to him:

   I never turned in an assignment but I have a cabin at the lake.

8. Another way of "softening" speech acts is to use a performative verb but to hedge it with a modal auxiliary:

   I want to ask you to sit over there.
   I must ask you to sit over there.

   Do these allow the Hearer the option of not taking them as direct acts (i.e., taking them literally)? If so, how do they convey the act of Requesting? Why doesn't *want* work with Offers that the Hearer can be expected to accept? Why doesn't *must* work with Offers?

9. The word *last* seems to involve the notion of relevant parameter. Consider the two ways to read

   Your last paper will be read by the Chairman.
   This is my last drink.

   Should we postulate as many senses of *last* as there are differentiable parameters, or leave the parameter vague ('than which there are no others'), to be filled in by information shared in context?

10. What "component" must a verb have to yield a "reversative" sense with *un-* or *de/dis-*?

untie	vs. *unsmoke	demagnetize vs.	?decirculate
undress	*unswim	devoice	*dissubsidize
		disconnect	

    Are there nonexistent combinations that show the condition(s) to be only necessary, not sufficient?

Conclusion:
What Semantics Was

Modern linguists assume that meanings can be represented in some fashion just as sounds can be represented in a phonetic alphabet and that a grammar of a language should enumerate the rules that enable speakers of the language to match certain Semantic Representations to certain Phonetic Representations. Generative grammar postulated the existence of Semantic Representations: linguists began to suggest what they might look like. How speakers relate the Semantic Representation to the world of things and relations was implicitly or explicitly considered a matter for psychology. The Semantic Representation of a sentence was given in an artificial language, like that of symbolic logic, with primitive terms (components or "features") and certain combinatorial principles (parentheses). A sentence was said to be given a *semantic interpretation* when it was given a Semantic Representation—i.e., translated into a formula of the semantic "language."

Few thought very much about how the components themselves were interpreted in terms of the world. If, for example, the Semantic Language postulated components such as EXT and MAX EXT, these were presumed to be primitive concepts and percepts, and the process by which one picks out that entity in the world might be briefly and informally described but was considered outside the province of semantics. Again, if analysis postulated a primitive term RED or SHALLOW, how that judgment was made of particular objects was a matter for theories of perception and cognition.

Logicians found this use of the term *semantic interpretation* very strange, since it amounted to what they customarily called *translation*. *Semantic interpretation* (or *semantics*) for a logician is precisely this second stage: the specification of the relation of the terms and formulas of the artificial language to the world. The logician objects that a formal language is meaningless unless the principles by which it makes contact with the world are specified. One can show interrelation of terms (similarities, entailments, equivalences, and contradictions) in any artificial language, but one has not at that point said anything about their "meaning"—how sentences can express true and false propositions about states of affairs in the world. Components express conditions that must be satisfied in the world for a sentence to be true in that world, but how does one determine whether those conditions are satisfied?

Linguists have come to recognize and concede the force of these objections. The need for a theory of reference (or *interpretation*, as the logicians use the term) is apparent, though there is no consensus on what such a theory should look like. In practice, some principles have been suggested couched as procedures for finding referents. Analyzing a term into components breaks the referent-finding procedure down into subprocedures—though rather artificially. If the sense of *boy* is given as HUMAN & MALE & NOT MATURE, then there are three determinations to be made, though the actual procedures would probably overlap here (i.e., MALE determined in relation to HUMAN, NOT MATURE partially in relation to MALE). Also (in practice) one might be content with clues not directly coded by the definitional components (does he act like a boy? dress like a boy?). In fact, the line between a referential (or interpretive) procedure and a definitional component is hard to draw: some define MALE as HAVING SEX ORGANS FOR BEGETTING PROGENY—or is this a referential procedure? (A definition is said to be operationalized when the outcome of some referential procedure is the sole criterion—"acid is what turns litmus paper red." How are the senses we have described operationalized—or are they?) It is through this contact with reality that material can become associated with words, or semanticized as a new sense: "Leslie is a boy no more —he shaved for the first time today."

Quantifiers force us to recognize the problem of interpretation, because their senses are almost or wholly instructions for determining the reference of the noun phrases they quantify. Thus Zeno Vendler (1967) suggests a sense for *any*: 'choose any you wish . . .', hence, by the way, *any* entails the existence of *some* referent:

?Any electric picture frame is unheard of in these parts.

?Any perpetual-motion machine has never been patented.

The component DISTRIBUTED suggested in Chapter VI to distinguish *every* from *all* is in essence a referential instruction ("check each one . . . ") that happens to interact with total readings. Representing the senses of quantifiers or connectives in terms of symbols of another language is only a notational convenience—it doesn't break out of the circle.

Once we recognize that quantifiers express referential instructions, the peculiar properties of generic sentences can be seen as a consequence of general referential protocols that happen to give results similar to those produced by more explicit instructions (quantifiers). This is the position of Nunberg and Pan (1975), who hold that

The boys kissed the girls.

means 'enough to sustain the generalization', where that standard is understood in context. In other sentences, it is 'enough to matter':

The Nazis tortured their prisoners.

Here it is not necessarily claimed that even a majority of Nazis did it, or a majority of prisoners got it. The sense is often paraphrasable by the curious modal operator *might well*: 'If some were Nazis and others were prisoners, they might well have tortured them.' Nunberg and Pan argue that

A gentleman is courteous.

amounts to a claim about all gentlemen, because in order to be suitable to test the truth of the proposition on, a given individual must have the properties of a gentleman. Since courtesy is one such property, by virtue of his being a suitable referent for *gentleman* he will have that property. We then have a case of virtual identity of reference without identity of sense (*even prime/square root of four*).

The importance of the notion of 'sufficient amount' extends well beyond generic sentences. Somehow we learn conventions that govern how much of something one must do to qualify for having done it. To be said to touch a table, one need only touch a small portion of it, but to be said to eat an apple, one must eat most of it. How much of the daily newspaper must you read to be said to have read it? How many breaks are allowed before it is false to say "I worked all day long"? These problems are touched by Kempson (1975) and Wilson (1975), who agree that they are not semantic problems, but they must certainly be central to a theory of reference.

The lack of a referential model strikes at the very heart of linguistic semantics—viz. the notion of entailment. To define S_1 as entailing S_2 in terms of the truth of S_2 over the same range of situations that S_1 is true over, we have to be able to specify the range of reference of each. The reader will recall the "shading" examples in Chapter I, e.g.,

They smeared paint on the wall.
They smeared the wall with paint.

I teach arithmetic to the little monsters.
I teach the little monsters arithmetic.

How can we decide whether these do refer to the same range of events? The literature in semantics of the last ten years is littered with exploded entailments and equivalences advanced by serious and intelligent men and to some degree still the subject to dispute. Still, it is important to ask, "How could they have made the 'mistakes'?"

In a recently reported study, Shenaut (1975) asked subjects to rate sentences for "degree of contradictoriness" and got ratings of "somewhat contradictory" for

It isn't Jack who Betty lives with, because she doesn't (even) live with anyone.

This and similar data led Shenaut to propose the notion of "sort-of entails" as a primitive notion of (fuzzy) semantics. One hopes that the subjects ("members of introductory classes in language for education majors at Boston University") did not grasp the meaning of the instructions or were being obedient in the performance of an initiatory ritual. One fears, however, that they had no very clear and distinct intuitions about entailment and contradiction. Wilson (1975) reports what may be somewhat more sophisticated responses to similar sentences: "A common reaction of informants to these sentences is first to reject them as contradictory, and then to accept them with varying degrees of alacrity when asked to construe them as denials of a prior statement" (p. 51). Adrienne Lehrer (1975) discusses judgments with certain adverbs that suggest the need for a "fuzzy" scale of entailment ranging from strict logical entailment to invited inference. The model of core (definitional) components and penumbral (associated) components may represent a possible sorting out of what are for most speakers fairly jumbled assortments of components mixed with referential clues (some loose but effective: "A truck is a vehicle only part of which is a passenger compartment"), cross-referenced and accessed as much by associative networks as by shared, entailed components.

The concepts and procedures described in these chapters, then, represent possible orderings of our knowledge, which appear rather highly idealized in the direction of "secondary-process" thinking. Semantics is not really in the infant stage—it is just now outgrowing its adolescent verities—and what we may hope to see are more realistic and natural, if fragmentary and fuzzy, accounts of what people actually mean when they say.

Glossary

(The numbers are chapter and section where the term is principally used.)

accent (7.2): Following Bolinger in a series of articles (most recently 1972a), I use the term *accent* here for 'most prominent syllable in the sentence', which is semantically the **focus** (q.v.). It is the peak of the intonation contour ('falling tone' in Quirk et al., 1972). Other accents are possible in more complicated situations (i.e., two foci in the same sentence)—these are discussed in Jackendoff (1972) and Quirk et al. (1972). I assume, following Schmerling (1974a, b) that the notion of "normal accent" is not well defined, but the interested reader should examine the arguments.

achievement verbs (2.3, 3.2): Achievements are one class of verb described by Zeno Vendler (1967). They are not actions and are incompatible with *for some time* adverbials:

He noticed the house (? for a few minutes).
    reached
    finished

When in the progressive, they mean 'is about to' and hence entail 'has not yet'. In (2.3), "group II" inchoatives are a subset of Achievements.

Achievements contrast with Accomplishments, which take both *for some time* and *in some time* adverbials and in the progressive mean 'is in process of doing':

He built a house.
He walked to town.

Both of these contrast with Activities, where the *in some time* adverbials are impossible:

He walked.

affix (3.1): A stretch of sounds attached to a stem or root is an affix. When prefixed, it is a *prefix*, when suffixed, a *suffix*. When the affix has a sense that, combined with the sense of the root, yields the meaning of the larger word, it is sometimes called a *lexeme* (e.g., *re-* in *reanalyze*); when it does not have such a sense (e.g., *re-* in *receive*), it may be called a morpheme to which no lexeme corresponds. That is, both *reanalyze* and *receive* can be segmented into two morphemes (units of structure), but only the former into two lexemes.

agent 5.1): Verbs described in Section 2.3 as having the component ACTION cast their Subjects in the role of Agent.

ambiguous: Except in Section 4.2, this term is used for lexical ambiguity (readings differing in regard to the senses of words) as opposed to syntactic or constructional ambiguity, which appears in (i) and (ii):

(i) He hit the man with the fedora.
(ii) The shooting of the guardsmen was atrocious.

In (i), the prepositional phrase *with the fedora can* be viewed as in construction with *the man* or as in construction with *hit*. In (ii), the Subject *the shooting of the guardsmen* can be viewed as derived from either 'guardsmen shoot' or '(one) shoot guardsmen'. Ambiguity must be distinguished from vagueness: a sentence is vague on some point when it simply gives no information: e.g., *He hammered the coat hanger* is vague with respect to the resulting state of the coat hanger, not ambiguous. (See Zwicky and Sadock, 1973.)

anomalous (Chapter II): Phrases and sentences that lack any reading are anomalous. Anomaly results when the selectional features of one member of the construction are not satisfied by the member in construction with it (e.g., *hydraulic sorrow*). Anomaly differs from contradiction or contradictory statement in that the incompatibility does not amount to a direct clash with a definitional component, as is the case with the latter. If one is willing to define **contradictory** (q.v.) as 'not capable of being true in any possible world', then anomalous sentences could be called contradictory.

associated component (see **definitional**)

benefactive (Chapter V, Table 1; implicitly in Chapter II, Exercise 4): Benefactive is suggested as a semantic role by some writers. Its central sense is 'one benefitted':

He made a cake *for Mary*/He made *Mary* a cake.
He did the dishes *for Mary*/*He did Mary the dishes.

Note that only the "for Mary to have" type allows the Beneficiary (or Benefactive) to appear as a Direct Object. The "benefit" may be negative, in which case the usual preposition marking the role is *on*:

John's class walked out on him.

The ancient grammatical term *ethical dative* is sometimes used for this relation.

case grammar: Case grammar is a linguistic model using semantic relational roles (Agent, Patient, etc.) as primitive terms rather than grammatical relations (Subject, Direct Object) or phrase-structure configurations.

causative: Verbs are called causative when they are transitive and entail a change in the condition or location of the Direct Object brought about by the action of the Subject:

He broke the window (into splinters).
He flattened the pipe.
He killed the spider.
He put a hammer on the shelf.

Usually verbs that express causation of a process are also called causative (*he spun the wheel*), as well as those that express the maintenance of a state (*prevent, keep, hold*). The term *permissive-causative* is sometimes used for such verbs as *drop, release*:

He dropped the iron on Mary's foot.
They released the irradiated males.

comitative (5.5): Comitative is suggested as a semantic role (Fillmore, 1966/69), or a product of conjunction, or a subtype of Instrument (Walmsley, 1971):

He went to the movies *with Harriet*.

component (1.4): Component is used here to represent concepts and is roughly equivalent to the terms *semantic feature* or *marker* (Katz, various publications), *category* (Gruber, 1967), or (*abstract*) *predicate* (in G. and R. Lakoff, McCawley, various publications).

connective (Chapter VI): The term is taken from logic, where it includes the symbols translated by *and, but, or* (conjunctions) and *if . . . then* (and by other words also). Connectives are held to be predicates by some, but not by logicians, because predicates combine with arguments to form propositions, but connectives combine propositions to form larger propositions.

connotation: This term is avoided in this work, because it is used by some to refer to emotional attitudes associated with words, by others to associated components.

contradiction   (1.2): A sentence expressing a proposition that is false in all possible worlds is a contradiction: *My brother is an only child*, where *only child* could never be truly predicated of an individual referred to by *my brother*. Katz distinguishes contradictions from contradictory sentences —the latter are inconsistent predications: *He inadvertently perjured himself*.

definitional   (1.5): Those components expressing properties or conditions entailed by the use of a word are said to be definitional for the word, or definitionally associated with the word. Associated components are not entailed, but do serve to distinguish word senses, including the 'semantic implications' of Wilson (1975) and 'conventional implicatures' of Grice (1975). Including associated components means that semantics goes beyond enumerating the truth-conditions of sentences.

degree-inchoatives (2.3, 3.2, 4.2): These are inchoative verbs that mean 'become more ADJ' and are compatible with *for some time* adverbials (which Achievements usually are not):

Prices rose for two months.

These are called "group I" inchoatives in (2.3).

deixis (7.1): Deixis is a term coined from Greek roots to refer to "pointing" in language to elements in the situation of utterance, either to Speaker, Hearer, or others, or time relative to that of utterance, or place relative to Speaker (and/or Hearer).

denotation (4.1): Denotation is the set of things or states of affairs referred to (denoted) by a word. Other terms are *extension* or *reference* (see Lyons, 1968). (See **referent**.)

entails (1.2): The definition is that of "weak" entailment in that it is not required that when S_2 is false, S_1 be false also. This detail is of little consequence in this book, except in Chapter VI, example (12), where strong → is meant.

equivalence (1.2): The logical definition of identical truth-conditions is the one used here.

extended sense: Extended sense is used here for both (1) a "figurative" or broadened sense recognized in a dictionary (1.6), or (2) a nonce extension one might make (2.5).

factitive (object) (5.3): The central sense is 'that which comes into existence as a result of the action of a (causative) verb'. It is not to be confused with the "cognate object" of an "accomplishment" verb (*run a race, sing a song*).

factive (1.2): A verb or adjective taking a complement sentence and entailing the truth of the complement sentence: *Othello knows that she is unfaithful*. Factives have been said to presuppose the truth of the complement—for arguments against this, see Wilson (1975).

feature (see **component**)

focus (7.2): Focus is defined here in semantic terms as the most significant piece of new information. It is marked in speech by the accent. The definition needs to be extended to allow two foci in certain instances.

gapping (1.2): Gapping is regarded in transformational grammar as a process deleting a verb (and adjoining material) in a conjoined sentence when it is identical in sense to a verb (and adjoining material) to its left: *Harry picked the lock with a knife, and Mary (   ), with a hairpin.*

gradable (3.2): Gradable is a term used by Edward Sapir (1949), later by Bolinger (1972) and after him by Quirk et al. (1972), meaning 'modifiable for degree or extent'. It applies to nouns and verbs as well as adjectives. Relative adjectives are a subset of the gradable adjectives.

grammar: This term is used variously by writers to mean (1) syntax, (2) the entire set of rules of a language mapping semantic structures onto strings of words, (3) the formal representation of those rules.

idiom (2.1, 3.1): The best definition is Weinreich's (1966, 1969): a mutually sense-selecting construction, where each member has a sense that is possible only in construction with the other item. The more common definition is: a construction whose reading is not the composition of any of the usual senses of its members. A usual example is *kick the bucket*, where the reading is very remote from usual senses of *kick* and *bucket*, but this need not be the case: the special senses can be more closely related to other senses (*throw a fit*). The term *semi-idiom* is used here for a construction where one member has the relevant sense only in construction with the other member(s), but the other(s) has a usual sense: *blade of grass, white lie.*

inchoative (2.3, 4.2): 'Involving a change of condition or location of the Subject (or Direct Object in causatives)'. Entails 'result after t' and 'result not immediately before t'

inverse (4.1): Two terms are said to be inverse when $aTb \equiv bT'a$:

a PARENT $b \equiv b$ CHILD a
a LARGER than $b \equiv b$ SMALLER than a

A single term is said to be symmetrical or reciprocal when $aTb \equiv bTa$ (*spouse, sibling*). The term *converse* is often used for what is called inverse here.

meaning postulate: The entailments of words can be listed as axioms associated with the word instead of components listed directly (as here):

kill: x KILL $y \rightarrow x$ CAUSE (y DIE)

This avoids the claim that 'CAUSE DIE' is the meaning of *kill* which it seems not to be—the element of direct action by the 'killer' is missing—

see Chapter I, Exercise 14. The complete set of meaning postulates would give an implicit definition of the word.

nativism (5.1): In regard to semantics, nativism is the belief that some concepts are innate and hence universal.

opaque (contexts) (6.1): Referentially opaque contexts are those in which a noun phrase need not be taken as referring to some existing thing (i.e., may not have a referent). These contexts include *not*, modal auxiliaries, generics, and verbs of wanting, seeking, etc.

paraphrase (Chapter I): Two constructions are paraphrases of each other when they have the same meaning. Logical equivalence is necessary for, but not sufficient to guarantee, it. Usually the term *synonymy* is restricted to such a relation between (the senses of) single words.

perfect tense (7.1): Perfect tense (also called perfect aspect) refers to the form *have* (or *had*) + Perfect Participle of the verb. In English, perfect tense does not have directly to do with perfected or completed action.

performative (7.3) A performative is a verb that, when used with *I* as its Subject, *you* as Direct Object, and in present tense, performs a speech act and says that it does. Sometimes the term is used for an abstract indicator of illocutionary force:

(I INFORM YOU THAT) You are liable to prosecution.
WARN
etc.

presupposition: Many of the relations said to involve entailment in the text are said by various writers to involve a stronger relation called presupposition. Many mutually incompatible definitions of presupposition have been given. For a thorough analysis of the term as it has been used see Kempson (1975) or Böer and Lycan (1976).

quantifier (6.2): Semantically, quantifiers of natural language (*all, every, each, some, few, several, many, one, two*, etc.) specify the number or amount of the objects referred to by a noun phrase. Syntactically, they appear as determiners (*several boys*) or as pronominal heads of noun phrases (*several [of the boys]*). This syntactic distinction is not absolute, since there are intermediate forms (*a lot of, a bunch of, a good deal of*), as well as "piece of" partitives (2.1) and measure phrases (*a quart of*) (see Quirk et al., 1972, pp. 145–46). Quantifiers are sometimes treated as predicates, but most logicians fiercely resist this. This matter, as well as the syntax of quantifiers, is discussed in Stockwell et al. (1973).

referent: The object referred to by a noun phrase is its referent. The denotation of a noun phrase is the set of possible referents.

relative adjectives (4.1): A relative adjective is one the sense of which involves comparison to some reference set.

scope (4.2, Chapters VI, VII): Material understood to be modified by a modifier is the material within the scope of the modifier; material negated by not is in the scope of *not*. In logical notation, material to the right of a negative or quantifier is understood to be in its scope. In Chapter VII the material operated on by *only, even*, etc. is in the scope of *only, even*, etc.

selectional restriction (Chapter II): Selectional restrictions record the contextual requirements of senses of words—i.e., the way other words must be understood for the particular word to have a certain sense. They are noted by components enclosed in angled brackets ⟨   ⟩, as opposed to square brackets [   ], the latter representing the sense of the item, the ⟨   ⟩ representing the sense other items must have. Not all restrictions on cooccurrence are selectional (semantically based). Some combinations of words (called *collocations*) seem relatively fixed or restricted but without semantic motivation:

good likelihood	badly wanted
good possibility	?badly wished
?good probability	

(see Bolinger, 1975: 100ff.)

sense: A sense of a word is one of its discrete meanings. The "meaning of a word" is either the set of its senses or one of its senses. The term *reading* of a sentence is used here for an amalgamation of the senses of the words.

stative: In general, verbs that cannot occur in the progressive are said to be stative (*cost, resemble, weigh, entail, equal*). This deficiency correlates with the semantic property of referring to a static state of affairs ("state of being") with two classes of exceptions:

(i) perception and cognition verbs are uneasy with the progressive (e.g., *know, see, forget*), though these can refer to processes;

(ii) *stand, sit, lie, rest, stay* can be used with the progressive, although they refer to static states of affairs.

There are several other classes of verbs: actions, inchoatives, processes.

theme: Theme, as used by Halliday (1967, 1970) and, following him, Quirk et al., 1972), refers to the "psychological subject" of a sentence or "that which the rest of the message is about." It is always the first element in the sentence and is not always "old" or "given" or "known" information. Unfortunately, Kuno (1972) restricts the term *theme* to "old, predictable information" only. Hence *a man* in

A man got run over.

would not be a theme. In Kuno (1975), however, a distinction is made between predictable and unpredictable theme, the latter appearing in

What do your brothers do for a living?

Well, *John* teaches music at a high school and *Bill* works for an insurance company

word: The definition of *word* is problematic, though not so as to obscure the discussion in the text. Each pairing of sound with sense could be said to qualify as a word (if it can occur freely—not, that is, as an affix), in which case a "word" with several senses would actually be said to be several words. This definition departs from common usage, and the term *lexical item* is sometimes used with this meaning. If we think of a word as the item heading an entry in a dictionary, then most words will be clusters of lexical items. Dictionaries differ, however, in the criteria for starting a new entry. *WNC* starts one for each part of speech (*lock*$_n$, *lock*$_v$, etc.), but *AHD* and *RHCD* group different parts of speech under one entry. When two lexical items seem unrelated semantically (or historically) (*lock*$_n$ 'of hair' and *lock*$_n$ 'on door'), most dictionaries give them separate entries and they would be considered to be homonyms. Archibald Hill (1970) has a lucid discussion of these points. It is often objected that representing each "lexical item" as a unique pairing of sound, syntactic properties, and sense fails to capture the relatedness that leads us to the locution 'different senses of the same word', but various formal mechanisms for registering this relatedness have been suggested (see e.g. Jackendoff, 1975).

Answers to the
Exercises and Problems

1.1 Two senses of *coat* (1 and 4 in *AHD*). There are two different associated properties of *fish* here: 'drinks a lot', 'swims well'. A third possibility: 'cold, lacking in emotion', though unlikely, given knowledge of the referents.

1.2 $a \rightarrow b$; $b \nrightarrow a$.

1.3 (1) possible situation: his friend has moved, but he doesn't know where.
(2) *bring* includes a WITH component; *B*, but not *A*, would be possible if he sent them, or arranged to have them sent.
(3) various causes of inability besides lack of skill.

1.4 (3) is not LE. *thin*$_v$ only entails 'become thinner (than it was)' and might be used when paint is still quite thick.

1.5 Both include TAKE ILLEGALLY; *steal* includes in addition SURREPTITIOUSLY, but *rob* does not (except in the sense 'burgle')—rather it expresses a face-to-face confrontation (sense 1 in *AHD*). Hence *steal* is closer to *embezzle* and *pilfer* than is *rob*.

1.6   *X* sister-in-law *Y*: *X* female spouse of sibling of *Y* or *X* female sibling of spouse *Y*

$$X \text{ FEMALE } \& \left\{ \begin{array}{l} A\&B \text{ PARENT } C\&Y \text{ \& } X \text{ MARRIED } C \\ A\&B \text{ PARENT } C\&X \text{ \& } C \text{ MARRIED } Y \end{array} \right\}$$

1.7   If neither ERASABLE nor SOLID-CORE is understood as definitional (i.e., if the phrase is not contradictory), one wonders what the phrase would apply to that *pen* would not do as well for.

1.8   A redundant phrase has a word expressing a component that is definitionally included in the meaning of another word.

1.9   (a) No hedge seems necessary: the President does not lack any of the criteria for being called the chief executive.
      (b) Again, beagle does not lack any definitional or primary criteria for being called a dog.
      (c) Either Peter is a person—then the proper hedge would be *real*—or Peter is a pet skunk, and again no hedge would be required.
      (d) Whale lacks a number of primary criteria associated with mammals: hair, living on land.
      (e) One expects *fruit*, rather than *vegetable*, here, since tomatoes are thought of as having the secondary and characteristic properties of vegetables, but not the definitional ones.

1.10   It is possible for there to be identity of reference without identity of sense (cf. Morning Star/Evening Star). SPOTTED is definitional for *leopard* and determines whether one would call a beast a leopard or a panther. Hence the terms are not even logically equivalent.

1.11   With *gun*, the function of firing bullets seems definitional and the physical form and properties only associated. *Imitation* entails 'not gun' and the failure must be in some definitional property. If in addition it doesn't resemble a gun, it is odd to call it a gun (like 1.7). *Imitation* may suggest visual likeness, but the same is true of *imitation vanilla* and *imitation thunder*.

1.12   Variation is possible here. The notion of "assumption linkage" in Postal (1974:411) is consistent with the view taken in the text.

1.13

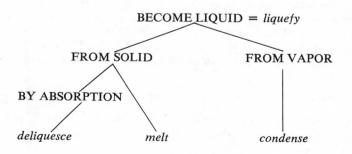

1.14 Most disputed with regard to logical equivalence. They are not paraphrases in that (a) conveys the notion of John's personal activity on Bill, while (b) could report the result of a train of events set off by John, but with someone or thing else actually doing the deed. (a) clearly entails (b); the question is whether (b) could be true and (a) said to be *false*. For a review of recent discussions, see Wierczbicka (1975).

1.15 They appear to be logically equivalent but not synonymous. On these, see Wilson (1975: Chapter 6).

2.1 (a) anomalous   (e) anomalous
         (b) contradiction   (f) contradiction
         (c) contradictory   (g) contradiction
         (d) anomalous

2.2 Roughly, CONTINGENT.

2.3 deteriorate—I   freeze—IIb (takes *completely* but not *slightly*)
        increase—I   forget—IIb (same)
        remember—obscure: in *remember him somewhat/slightly*, possibly 'somewhat of him', otherwise, pretty much IIa.

2.4 They appear to be distinguishing between a group I sense ('get larger') and a group II sense ('reach full size'), using *up* to distinguish them. The construction is a "resultative" and group I senses are strange with it—it usually induces a group II sense, but cf. *Their strength is somewhat diminished.*

2.5 Apparently so, as in most dictionaries.

2.6 The class is usually said to be that of ACTIONS.

2.7 Though so defined by Bartsch and Vennemann (1972) following Katz and Fodor (1963), it appears not to be so for most people, since one does hear people saying to recently divorced men, "How does it feel to be a bachelor again?"

2.8 *Cloud* normally is VISIBLE; in *cloud of fragrance*, one is inclined to adjust *fragrance* to 'fragrant vapor'; *cloud of suspicion* would seem to involve a similar adjustment, but this time on *cloud*, so that *invisible* would be almost redundant modifying it. It would be hard to specify a metaphorical extension for *invisible cloud* without a context. *After a cigarette*—here not metaphor, but the addition of components PERIOD SPENT CONSUMING . . . . *Three hours*—again added components 'time spent travelling'— see *AHD: hour.*

2.9 Some suggest: 'similar in shape to a loaf of bread'. Cooked? (See *WNC.*)

2.10 For (a), see introduction to Chapter VII. For (b), see McCawley (1971), where (2) are excluded for having "subjective" or "evaluative" results. See also Green (1972). No one has captured all of these, if indeed a generalization or set of them be possible.

2.11 There is a relation between precise physical characteristics and functions, obviously, but function looms large for most of these.

2.12 Apparently fainting is too sharp or sudden a process.

3.1
(a) coffee cream	(f) heart failure
(b) bug spray	(g) heart failure
(c) ash tray (?life boat)	(h) steam cleaning
(d) alcohol lamp	(i) washing machine
(e) candle light	(j) swimming pool

3.2 (a) must be ACTION
(b) cannot be STATIVE. In general largely actions, but cf. *changeable*.

3.3 (1) They make telescopic mirrors.
(2) Telescopic photographs of the Martian canals show many gaps.
(3) The telescopic stars vastly outnumber the visible ones.
(4) Superman had (has?) telescopic vision.
(5) The handle is telescopic and can be pressed entirely into the body.

3.4

abducive	4 a. informing	*egredient*	that which is
	5 b. distracting		2 a. smoothed
	0 c. conserving		3 b. held
			4 c. vaporized
supponent	5 a. fundamental	*arrective*	1 a. raising
	1 b. excessive		4 b. retarding
	2 c. softening		4 c. impairing
erigible	capable of being	*degressive*	8 a. going down
	2 a. twisted		0 b. coming up
	3 b. raised		1 c. turning around
	3 c. bent		

3.5 In the line: "But nothing did he dread, but ever was ydrad," *ydrad* might be the passivized form of *dread*: "He dreaded nothing, but was always dreaded."

4.1
(a)—type 3	(d)—type 7
(b)—type 2	(e)—type 4
(c)—type 5	(f)—type 6

4.2 They occur with inchoative (and causative) verbs. The meaning is '*V* at end of interval', not within it (as *in the night*). This may be because the interval is otherwise unbounded (contrast *the night*).

4.3 (a)—almost went, but got routed to Chicago instead.
—went almost to Boston.
(b)—(iterative) didn't keep waking up until dawn.
—(duration) didn't (once) wake up before dawn.

4.4 (a) Only an iterative reading (different loaves went stale), since duration-of-*V* is factually odd (doesn't take that long) as is duration-of-result (stays that way for the duration).

(b) Most likely duration-of-result, since *going out of one's mind* is regarded as a completable activity.

4.5 No. See Smith, Shoben, and Rips (1974).

5.1 (a) Agent   (d) Patient
(b) Patient (?Goal, ?recipient)   (e) Goal
(c) Instrument   (f) Patient; Source

5.2 (a) *John* as Patient, or as Agent
(b) *coat* as Patient, or as Instrument ('makes one warm')
(c) *milkshake* either Patient (with *her* as Beneficiary) or Factitive (with *her* as Patient)
(d) *John* as Experiencer or as Agent
(e) *John* as Experiencer or as Agent

5.3 (a) *cane* clearly Instrument
(b) *cane* clearly Patient—but is it Instrument also?

5.4 *To the party* doesn't seem to be a role related to *wear*. Fillmore (1974) suggests that the sentence is an "amalgam" of two sentences:

$$\text{She wore a green dress} \left\{ \begin{array}{c} \text{and} \\ \text{when} \end{array} \right\} \text{she went to the party.}$$

5.5 In (c), (1) and (2) are very close. Sentences from Anderson (1971a).

6.1 For *three . . . two*, two readings: (a) each of them killed two (six dead), (b) they bagged two in all. For *two . . . three*, the (b) reading strongly preferred.

6.2 The (b) sentence tends to be read with narrow ∀ quantifier scope: "There is one called mother that all men have," but the wide-scope tendency of *every* does not allow this reading in (a).

6.3 Many people say *no*: the situation where many arrows hit the target, but many didn't, is compatible with b), less so with (a). Again there are dialect differences.

6.4 *Because* leans toward *if* in not asserting a causal link between propositions. This may be relatable to its use as an adverbial connective of reason.

6.5 As discussed in the text, *if* can be taken as expressing a necessary as well as a sufficient condition (if not not operate, then not die). The *though* contrasts with this expectation. *And* is also possible if the expectation is less lively (i.e., in a conversation between doctors?).

6.6 Knowledge of the rules of baseball apparently (i.e., that there are other ways to be out.)

6.7 It looks that way, but see Nunberg and Pan (1975) and the Conclusion.

7.1 (a)—2   (c)—4
       (b)—3   (d)—1

7.2 See G. Lakoff (1971b), Schmerling (1974b). Lakoff suggests a belief in the situation:

$$V_1 \rightarrow V_2 \qquad \begin{array}{l} \text{(call one a virgin} \rightarrow \text{insult one)} \\ \text{(call one a virgin} \rightarrow \text{call one a liar)} \end{array}$$

For virgin/liar, imagine that Mary has been discoursing on the ecstasy of sex . . . .

7.3 Yes, in that each reading pairs with an accent:

murder—execute
the old woman—it was someone else
with a hammer—used an ax

7.4 (b) requires Hearer to provide information on his desires, while (a) allows him to respond to an order without saying that he wants more. The potential impoliteness of (b) is obvious if we imagine that the guest does indeed want more cake, and is hungrily eyeing it. (See R. Lakoff, 1972.)

7.5 Preconditions (Searle, 1969):
(a) Hearer believes *P* may occur.
(b) Hearer would not find *P* in his interest.
(c) Speaker believes that *P* will come about.
(d) Speaker believes that *P* would not be in Hearer's interest.

In general, questioning a Hearer-based condition, or stating a Speaker-based condition, conveys the act.

7.6 (d) is very impolite, since it imposes fact and value-judgment on the Hearer. (b) is also impolite, as it directly requires exposure of Hearer's feelings, though it is less impolite than (d), because it does not assume that the Hearer is opposed. (a) and (c) are relatively more polite, and (a) probably more than (c), since an opinion is not much of a personal revelation, while giving an opinion is potentially an imposition:

+polite   (a) (c) (b) (d)   −polite

7.7 Assuming final grades are not in, the teacher might assume that, since the first conjunct gives a reason to fail and the second is contrasted with it, the second represents in the Speaker's mind a reason not to fail. This might be the case if

(1) it represents great power and wealth that could menace the teacher (i.e., an indirect threat);

(2) it represents a potential benefit to the teacher, assuming the student's continued good will (i.e., an Offer to bribe).

7.8 Yes, they can be taken literally, with replies "Please don't" or "Don't bother." They convey the acts by the principles of Expression of Desire (where cooperation seems to be minimally permission to Request) and Asserted Obligation: "A Speaker who asserts that he is under some obligation to act in a certain way may be inferred to intend to act in that way." Since it doesn't make sense to request permission to do something that is in the Hearer's interest, the indirectness of *I want to offer to help you* seems pointless (or sinister—there are some strings attached to my help?). Since *must* dissociates Speaker from the obligation, it seems strange to dissociate oneself from an Offer—the impression is of an unwilling offer. (See Fraser, 1974.)

7.9 The ambiguity (if that is the right word), of course, has to do with *last* as 'most recent' or as 'final (in some understood progression)'. If one takes 'most recent' as the least contextually specified interpretation (i.e., 'final in series of events until now'), then we could argue that the interpretations do not reflect multiple senses of *last*. Note that the 'most recent' interpretation depends on the noun's being interpreted as referring to an "event"— 'paper (which you have written)', 'drink (which I was served or drinking)'. On the other hand, if this kind of multiple interpretation occurs only with *last,* perhaps it may be regarded as a distinguishable sense.

7.10 The conditions would seem to be that verbs must be "change" verbs (i.e., inchoative) and the change referred to must be able to be undone (i.e., the object brought back to its initial state). The latter condition appears in the badness of *unpaint,* where the action of stripping paint apparently does not get the object back to its pristine state. However, an alternative view would be that the action of reversing must be thought of as roughly similar to the initial action. This does not seem too attractive, however, since unravelling is quite differently done than ravelling.

Bibliography

COLLECTIONS

CORUM, Claudia, T. Cedric SMITH-STARK, and Ann WEISER, eds. *Papers from the Ninth Regional Meeting of the Chicago Linguistic Society*, 1973.

DAVIDSON, Donald, and Gilbert HARMON, eds. *Semantics of Natural Language*. Dordrecht: D. Reidel Publishing Company, 1972.

FILLMORE, Charles J., and D. Terence LANGENDOEN, eds. *Studies in Linguistic Semantics*. New York: Holt, Rinehart, and Winston, Inc., 1971.

GROSSMAN, Robin E., L. James SAN, and Timothy J. VANCE, eds. *Papers from the Parasession on Functionalism*. Chicago Linguistic Society, 1975.

LA GALY, Michael W., Robert A. FOX, and Anthony BRUCK, eds. *Papers from the Tenth Regional Meeting of the Chicago Linguistic Society*, 1974.

MORGAN, Jerry, and Peter COLE, eds. *Syntax and Semantics*, Vol. III: *Speech Acts*. New York: Academic Press, 1975.

PERANTEAU, Paul M., Judith N. LEVI, and Gloria C. PHARES, eds. *Papers from the Eighth Regional Meeting of the Chicago Linguistic Society*, 1972.

STEINBERG, Danny D., and Leon A. JAKOBOVITS, eds. *Semantics: an Interdisciplinary Reader*. Cambridge, England: Cambridge University Press, 1971.

BOOKS AND PAPERS[1]

ABBOTT, Barbara. "Some Problems in Giving an Adequate Model-theoretical Account of CAUSE," in *Berkeley Studies in Syntax and Semantics*, Vol. I, ed. Charles J. FILLMORE, George LAKOFF, and Robin LAKOFF. Berkeley: Department of Linguistics: University of California, 1974.

ADAMS, Karen, and Nancy Faires CONKLIN. "Toward a Theory of Natural Classification," in CORUM et al., pp. 1–10.

ADAMS, Valerie. *An Introduction to Modern English Word-Formation*. London: Longman, 1973.

ANDERSEN, Elaine. "Cups and Glasses: Learning that Boundaries are Vague," *Journal of Child Language*, 2 (1975), 79–103.

ANDERSON, John M. *The Grammar of Case: Towards a Localistic Theory*. Cambridge, England: Cambridge University Press, 1971(a).

————, "Remarks on the Hierarchy of Quasi-Predications," *Revue Roumaine de Linguistique*, 17 (1971b), 23–44; 121–40; 193–202; 319–35.

————. "Ghosts of Time Past," *FL.*, 9 (1973), 481–91.

————. *An Essay on Aspect*. The Hague: Mouton, 1973(b).

ANDERSON, Stephen R. "How to Get *Even*," *Lg.*, 48 (1972), 893–906.

ANGLIN, J. M. *The Growth of Word Meaning*. Cambridge, Mass.: MIT Press, 1970.

AUSTIN, John L. *How to Do Things With Words*. Oxford: Oxford University Press, 1962.

BABCOCK, Sandra Scharff. "Periphrastic Causatives," *FL.*, 8 (1972), 30–43.

BALLARD, Lee, Robert CONRAD, and Robert LONGACRE. "The Deep and Surface Grammar of Interclausal Relations," *FL.*, 7 (1971), 70–118.

BARTSCH, Renate. *Adverbial Semantics*. New York: North Holland/American Elsevier, forthcoming.

————, and Theo VENNEMANN. *Semantic Structures*. Frankfurt: Athenäum Verlag, 1972.

BEARDSLEY, Monroe C. "The Metaphorical Twist," *Philosophy and Phenomenological Research*, 22 (1962), 293–307.

BENDIX, Edward H. *Componential Analysis of General Vocabulary*. Indiana University Research Center in Anthropology, Folklore, and Linguistics, Publication 41, 1966.

BENNETT, David C. *Spatial and Temporal Uses of English Prepositions*. London: Longman, 1975.

BIERWISCH, Manfred. "Semantics," in *New Horizons in Linguistics*, ed. John LYONS. Harmondsworth: Penguin Books, Ltd., 1970.

————. "On Classifying Semantic Features," in STEINBERG and JAKOBOVITS.

[1]*Foundations of Language (FL), Journal of Linguistics (JL), Language (Lg).*

BLACK, Max. "Metaphor," in *Models and Metaphors*. Ithaca: Cornell University Press, 1962.

BÖER, Steven E., and William G. LYCAN. "The Myth of Semantic Presupposition," Ohio State Working Papers in Linguistics, no. 19 (1976) and available from Indiana University Linguistics Club.

BOLINGER, Dwight. "The Atomization of Meaning," *Lg.*, 41 (1965), 555–73.

————. "Adjectives in English: Attribution and Predication," *Lingua*, 18 (1967), 1–34.

————. 'Semantic Overloading: A Restudy of the Verb *remind*," *Lg.*, 47 (1971), 522–47.

————. *Degree Words*. The Hague: Mouton, 1972.

————. "Accent is Predictable (If You're a Mind-reader)," *Lg.*, 48 (1972a), 633–44.

————. *Aspects of Language* (2d ed.). New York: Harcourt Brace Jovanovich, Inc., 1975.

BOWERMAN, Melissa. *Early Syntactic Development: A Cross-linguistic Study with Special Reference to Finnish*. Cambridge, England: Cambridge University Press, 1973.

BROWN, Roger. "The First Sentences of Child and Chimpanzee," in *Psycholinguistics: Selected Papers*. New York: The Free Press, 1970.

————. *A First Language: The Early Stages*. Cambridge, Mass.: Harvard University Press, 1973.

BUCKINGHAM, Hugh. "The Comitative and Case Grammar," *FL.*, 10 (1973), 111–22.

CAMPBELL, Robin N., and Roger WALES. "Comparative Structures in English," *JL.*, 5 (1969), 215–51.

————. "The Study of Language Acquisition," in *New Horizons in Linguistics*, ed. John LYONS. Harmondsworth: Penguin Books, Ltd., 1970.

CARDEN, Guy. "Dialect Variation and Abstract Syntax," in *Some New Directions in Linguistics*, ed. Roger W. SHUY. Washington: Georgetown University Press, 1974.

CHAFE, Wallace L. *Meaning and the Structure of Language*. Chicago: Chicago University Press, 1970.

————. "Language and Memory," *Lg.*, 49 (1973), 261–81.

————. "Language and Consciousness," *Lg.*, 50 (1974), 111–33.

CHAPIN, Paul G. "Review of Stockwell et al.: *The Major Syntactic Structures of English*," *Lg.*, 48 (1972), 645–67.

CHOMSKY, Noam. "Deep Structure, Surface Structure, and Semantic Interpretation," in STEINBERG and JAKOBOVITS.

————. "Remarks on Nominalization," in *Readings in English Transformational Grammar*, ed. Roderick JACOBS and Peter ROSENBAUM. Waltham, Mass.: Xerox College Publishing, 1971(b).

CLARK, Eve V. "What's in a Word? On the Child's Acquisition of Semantics in His First Language," in *Cognitive Development and the Acquisition of Language*, ed. T. E. MOORE. New York: Academic Press, 1973.

————. "Normal States and Evaluative View-points," *Lg.*, 50 (1974), 316–32.

————, and Olga K. GARNICA. "Is He Coming or Going? On the Acquisition of Deictic Verbs," *Journal of Verbal Learning and Verbal Behavior*, 13 (1974), 559–72.

————, and C. J. SENGUL. "Deictic Contrasts in Language Acquisition." Paper read at the LSA Winter Meeting (New York), 1974.

CRUSE, D. A. "Some Thoughts on Agentivity," *JL.*, 9 (1973), 11–24.

DILLON, George L. "Perfect and Other Aspects in a Case Grammar of English," *JL.*, 9 (1973), 271–79.

————. "Some Postulates Characterizing Volitive NPs," *JL.*, 10 (1974), 221–33.

————. "Passives and Reflexives as Quasi-Predications," *Edinburgh Working Papers in Linguistics*, forthcoming.

DONALDSON, Margaret. *A Study of Children's Thinking*. London: Tavistock, 1963.

————, and Roger WALES. "On the Acquisition of Some Relational Terms," in *Cognition and the Development of Language*, ed. John R. HAYES. New York: John Wiley & Sons, Inc., 1970.

DOWTY, David R. "On the Syntax and Semantics of the Atomic Predicate CAUSE," in PERANTEAU et al.

————. *Studies in the Logic of Verb Aspect and Time Reference in English.* Austin: Department of Linguistics, University of Texas, 1972(b).

DREYFUSS, Gail Raimi, Manfred KOCHEN, Jane ROBINSON, and Albert BADRE. "On the Psycholinguistic Reality of Fuzzy Sets," in GROSSMAN et al.

FILLMORE, Charles J. "Towards a Modern Theory of Case," in *Modern Studies in English*, ed. David REIBEL and Sanford SCHANE. Englewood Cliffs, N.J.: Prentice-Hall, Inc., 1969 (first published 1966).

————. "The Case for Case," in *Universals in Linguistic Theory*, ed. Emmon BACH and Robert T. HARMS. New York: Holt, Rinehart, and Winston, Inc., 1968.

————. "Lexical Entries for Verbs," *FL.*, 4 (1968b), 373–93.

————. "Review of E. Bendix: *Componential Analysis of General Vocabulary*," *General Linguistics*, 9 (1969), 41–65.

————. "Types of Lexical Information," in STEINBERG and JAKOBOVITS (also published in 1970).

————. "Some Problems for Case Grammar," in *Georgetown Monograph Series in Language and Linguistics*, no. 24, ed. Richard J. O'BRIEN. Washington: Georgetown University Press, 1971.

————. "Verbs of Judging," in FILLMORE and LANGENDOEN (= 1971a).

————. "Subjects, Speakers, and Roles," in DAVIDSON and HARMON.

————. "May We Come In?" *Semiotica*, 9 (1973), 97–116.

————. "The Future of Semantics," in *Berkeley Studies in Syntax and Semantics*, Vol. I, ed. Charles FILLMORE, George LAKOFF, and Robin LAKOFF. Berkeley: Department of Linguistics, University of California, 1974.

FODOR, Janet Dean. "Like-Subject Verbs and Causal Clauses in English," *JL.*, 10 (1974), 95–110.

————, J. A. FODOR, and M. F. GARRETT. "The Psychological Unreality of Semantic Representations," *Linguistic Inquiry*, 6 (1975), 515–31.

FRASER, Bruce. "An Analysis of 'even' in English," in FILLMORE and LANGENDOEN.

————. "Hedged Performatives," in MORGAN and COLE.

FRIEDRICH, Paul. "Shape Categories in Grammar," *Linguistics*, 77 (1972), 5–21.

GEIS, Michael. "*If* and *Unless*," in *Issues in Linguistics: Papers in Honor of Henry and Renee Kahane*, ed. Braj B. KACHRU, Robert B. LEES, Yakov MALKIEL, Angelina PIETRANGELI, and Sol SAPORTA. Urbana: University of Illinois Press, 1973.

————, and Arnold ZWICKY. "On Invited Inference," *Linguistic Inquiry*, 2 (1971), 561–66.

GIVÓN, Talmy. "Notes on the Semantic Structure of English Adjectives," *Lg.*, 46 (1970), 816–37.

————. "The Time-Axis Phenomenon," *Lg.*, 49 (1973), 890–925.

GLEITMAN, Lila, and Henry GLEITMAN. *Phrase and Paraphrase*. New York: W. W. Norton & Company, Inc., 1970.

GORDON, David, and George LAKOFF. "Conversational Postulates," in *Papers from the Seventh Regional Meeting of the Chicago Linguistic Society, 1971*. Also in MORGAN and COLE.

GREEN, Georgia M. "Some Observations on the Syntax and Semantics of Instrumental Verbs," in PERANTEAU et al.

————. *Semantics and Syntactic Regularity*. Bloomington: Indiana University Press, 1974.

GRICE, H. Paul. "Logic and Conversation," in MORGAN and COLE.

GRUBER, Jeffrey. *Functions of the Lexicon in Formal Descriptive Grammars* (originally 1967; available from the Indiana University Linguistics Club).

HALLIDAY, M. A. K. "Notes on Transitivity and Theme in English," *JL.*, 3 (1967), 37–81; 199–244; and 4 (1968), 179–215.

————. "Language Structure and Language Function," in *New Horizons in Linguistics*, ed. John LYONS. Harmondsworth: Penguin Books, Ltd., 1970.

HARRIS, Martin. "Some Problems for a Case Grammar of Latin and Early Romance," *JL.*, 11 (1975), 183–93.

HAVILAND, Susan, and Eve V. CLARK. " 'This man's father is my father's son': A Study of the Acquisition of English Kin Terms," *Journal of Child Language*, 1 (1974), 23–47.

HILL, Archibald A. "Laymen, Lexicographers, and Linguists," *Lg.*, 46 (1970), 245–58.

HORN, Laurence. "A Presuppositional Analysis of *only* and *even,*" in *Papers from the Fifth Regional Meeting of the Chicago Linguistic Society*, ed. Robert I. BINNICK, Alice DAVISON, Georgia M. GREEN, and Jerry L. MORGAN. Chicago: Department of Linguistics, University of Chicago, 1969.

HUDDLESTON, Rodney D. 'Some Remarks on Case Grammar," *Linguistic Inquiry*, 1 (1970), 501–11.

INGRAM, David. "Transitivity in Child Language," *Lg.*, 47 (1971), 888–910.

JACKENDOFF, Ray S. *Semantic Interpretation in Generative Grammar.* Cambridge, Mass.: MIT Press, 1972.

————. "Morphological and Semantic Regularities in the Lexicon," *Lg.*, 51 (1975), 639–71.

JOOS, Martin. "Semantic Axiom Number One," *Lg.*, 48 (1972), 257–65.

KARTTUNEN, Lauri. "Implicative Verbs," *Lg.*, 47 (1971), 340–58.

————. "The Logic of English Predicate Complement Constructions," (1971a, available from the Indiana University Linguistics Club).

————. "Possible and Necessary," in *Syntax and Semantics*, Vol. I, ed. John KIMBALL. New York: Seminar Press, 1972.

KASTOVSKY, Dieter. "Causatives," *FL.*, 10 (1973), 255–315.

KATZ, Jerrold J. *The Philosophy of Language.* New York: Harper & Row, Publishers, 1966.

————. *Semantic Theory.* New York: Harper & Row, Publishers, 1972.

————, and Jerry FODOR. "The Structure of a Semantic Theory," *Lg.*, 39 (1963), 170–210.

————, and R. NAGEL. "Meaning Postulates and Semantic Theory," *FL.*, 11 (1974), 311–40.

KEENAN, Edward L. "Two Kinds of Presupposition in Natural Language," in FILLMORE and LANGENDOEN.

KELLER-COHEN, Deborah. "Cognition and the Acquisition of Temporal Reference," in LaGALY et al.

KEMPSON, Ruth. *Presupposition and the Delimitation of Semantics.* Cambridge, England: Cambridge University Press, 1975.

KINTSCH, Walter. *The Representation of Meaning in Memory.* New York: John Wiley & Sons, Inc., 1974.

KIPARSKY, Paul, and Carol KIPARSKY. "Fact," in STEINBERG and JAKOBOVITS.

KITAGAWA, Chisato. "Purpose Expressions in English," *Lingua*, 34 1974), 31–46.

KLOOSTER, W. G. "Reduction in Dutch Measure Phrase Sentences," in *Generative Grammar in Europe*, ed. Ferenc KIEFER and Nicholas RUWET. Dordrecht: D. Reidel Publishing Company, 1972.

KÖNIG, E. "The Semantic Structure of Time Prepositions in English," *FL.*, 10 (1974), 551–63.

KORNFELD, Judith. "Some Insights into the Cognitive Representation of Word Meanings," in GROSSMAN et al.

KROCH, Anthony S. "The Semantics of Scope in English" (unpublished Ph.D. thesis, MIT, 1975; available from the Indiana University Linguistics Club).

KUNO, Susumo. "Functional Sentence Perspective," *Linguistic Inquiry*, 3 (1972), 269–320.

————. *The Structure of the Japanese Language*. Cambridge, Mass.: MIT Press, 1973.

————. "Three Perspectives in the Functional Approach to Syntax," in GROSSMAN et al.

LABOV, William. "The Boundaries of Words and Their Meanings," in *New Ways of Analyzing Variation in English*, ed. Charles-James N. BAILEY and Roger W. SHUY. Washington, D.C.: Georgetown University Press, 1973.

LAKOFF, George. *Irregularity in Syntax*. New York: Holt, Rinehart, and Winston, Inc., 1970.

————. "The Role of Deduction in Grammar," in FILLMORE and LANGENDOEN (= 1971a).

————. "Presupposition and Relative Well-formedness," in STEINBERG and JAKOBOVITS (= 1971b).

————. "Linguistics and Natural Logic," in DAVIDSON and HARMON (= 1972a).

————. "Hedges: a Study in Meaning Criteria and the Logic of Fuzzy Concepts," in PERANTEAU et al. (= 1972b).

LAKOFF, Robin. "If's, And's, and But's About Conjunction," in FILLMORE and LANGENDOEN.

————. "Language in Context," *Lg.*, 48 (1972), 907–27.

————. "The Logic of Politeness; or, Minding your Ps and Qs," in CORUM et al.

LANGENDOEN, D. Terence. *The Study of Syntax*. New York: Holt, Rinehart, and Winston, Inc., 1969.

LARKIN, Don, and Michael H. O'MALLEY. "Declarative Sentences and the Rule-of Conversation Hypothesis," in CORUM et al.

LAWLER, John. "Generic to a Fault," in PERANTEAU et al.

————. "Tracking the Generic Toad," in CORUM et al.

LEECH, Geoffrey N. *Towards a Semantic Description of English*. London: Longman, 1969.

————. *Semantics*. Harmondsworth: Penguin Books, Ltd., 1974.

LEE, Gregory. "Notes in Defense of Case Grammar," in *Papers from the Seventh Regional Meeting of the Chicago Linguistic Society* (= 1971a).

————. "Subjects and Agents, II," *Ohio State Working Papers in Linguistics* 7, (1971b).

LEES, Robert B. "Problems in the Grammatical Analysis of English Nominal Compounds," in *Progress in Linguistics*, ed. Manfred BIERWISCH and Karl Erich HEIDOLPH. The Hague: Mouton, 1970.

LEVI, Judith N. "Where Do All Those Other Adjectives Come From?" in CORUM et al.

————. "On the Alleged Idiosyncrasy of Non-predicate NPs," in LA GALY et al.

LEHRER, Adrienne. "Semantic Cuisine," *JL.*, 5 (1969), 39–55.

————. *Semantic Fields and Lexical Structure.* New York: North Holland/ American Elsevier, 1974.

————. 'Interpreting Certain Adverbs: Semantics or Pragmatics?" *JL.*, 11 (1975), 239–48.

LOEWENBERG, Ina. "Identifying Metaphors," *FL.*, 12 (1975), 315–38.

LYONS, John. *Introduction to Theoretical Linguistics.* Cambridge, England: Cambridge University Press, 1968.

MARCHAND, Hans. *Categories and Types of Present-day English Word-Formation* (2d ed.). Munich: C. H. Beck, 1969.

MATES, Benson. *Elementary Logic* (2d ed.). Oxford: Oxford University Press, 1972.

McCAWLEY, James D. "The Role of Semantics in a Grammar," in *Universals in Linguistic Theory*, ed. Emmon BACH and Robert T. HARMS. New York: Holt, Rinehart, and Winston, Inc., 1968.

————. "Tense and Time Reference in English," in FILLMORE and LANGEN-DOEN (= 1971a).

————. "Prelexical Syntax," in *Monograph Series in Languages and Linguistics*, no. 24, ed. Richard J. O'BRIEN. Washington: Georgetown University Press, 1971 (= 1971b).

MACNAMARA, John. "Parsimony and the Lexicon," *Lg.*, 47 (1971), 359–74.

MILLER, George A. "English Verbs of Motion: A Case Study in Semantics and Lexical Memory," in *Coding Processes in Human Memory*, ed. Arthur W. MELTON and Edwin MARTIN. New York: V. H. Winston & Sons and John Wiley & Sons, Inc., 1972.

MOHAN, Bernard A. "Principles, Postulates, Politeness," in LAGALY et al.

MORAVCSIK, J. M. E. "Review of Leech: *Towards a Semantic Description of English," Lg.*, 48 (1972), 445–53.

NELSON, Katherine. "Concept, Word, and Sentence . . . , " *Psych. Rev.*, 81 (1974), 267–85.

NIDA, Eugene A. *Componential Analysis of Meaning.* The Hague: Mouton, 1975.

NILSEN, Don Lee Fred. *The Instrumental Case in English.* The Hague: Mouton, 1973.

NUNBERG, Geoffrey, and Chiahua PAN. "Inferring Quantification in Generic Sentences," *Papers from the Eleventh Regional Meeting of the Chicago Linguistic Society*, ed. Robin E. GROSSMAN, L. James SAN, and Timothy VANCE.

PARTEE, Barbara, Sharon SABSAY, and John SOPER. "Bibliography: Logic and Language." Available from the Indiana University Linguistics Club.

PIAGET, Jean. *Judgment and Reasoning in the Child*, trans. Marjorie WARDEN. Totowa, N.J.: Littlefield, Adams, 1959.

———, Bärbel INHELDER, and Alina SZEMINSKA. *The Child's Conception of Geometry*, trans. E. A. SUNZER. New York: Basic Books, Inc., 1960.

POSTAL, Paul M. "On the Surface Verb 'remind'," *Linguistic Inquiry*, 2 (1970), 37–120 (also in FILLMORE and LANGENDOEN).

———. *On Raising*. Cambridge, Mass.: MIT Press, 1974.

QUIRK, Randolph, Sidney GREENBAUM, Geoffrey LEECH, and Jan SVARTVIK. *A Grammar of Contemporary English*. London: Longman, 1972.

REICHENBACH, Hans. *Elements of Symbolic Logic*. New York: The Free Press, 1947.

RIPS, Lance J., Edward J. SHOBEN, and Edward E. SMITH. "Performance Models of Semantic Composition," in GROSSMAN et al.

SADOCK, Jerrold. *Toward a Linguistic Theory of Speech Acts*. New York: Academic Press, Inc., 1974.

SAG, Ivan A., and Mark LIBERMAN. "The Intonational Disambiguation of Indirect Speech Acts," in *Papers from the Eleventh Regional Meeting of the Chicago Linguistic Society*, ed. Robin E. GROSSMAN, L. James SAN, and Timothy J. VANCE.

SAPIR, Edward. "Grading: A Study in Semantics," in *Selected Writings*, ed. D. G. MANDELBAUM. Berkeley and Los Angeles: University of California Press, 1949.

SCHACHTER, Paul. "On Syntactic Categories." Available from the Indiana University Linguistics Club.

SCHMERLING, Susan. "A Re-Examination of 'Normal Stress'," *Lg.*, 50 (1974a), 66–73.

———. "Contrastive Stress and Semantic Relations," in LAGALY et al.

SEARLE, John R. *Speech Acts*. Cambridge, England: Cambridge University Press, 1969.

SHATZ, Marilyn. "The Comprehension of Indirect Speech Acts: Can Two-year Olds Pass the Salt?" Paper read at the Summer LSA Meeting (Amherst), 1974.

SHENAUT, Greg. "Valves: Plumbing the Presuppositional Depths (or, What's a Plug Like You Doing in a Hole Like This?)," in *Papers from the Eleventh Regional Meeting of the Chicago Linguistic Society*, ed. Robin G. GROSSMAN, L. James SAN, and Timothy J. VANCE.

SLOBIN, Dan I. *Psycholinguistics*. Glenview, Ill.: Scott, Foresman and Company, 1971.

SMITH, Edward E., Edward J. SHOBEN, and Lance J. RIPS. "Structure and Process in Semantic Memory: A Featural Model for Semantic Decisions," *Psych. Rev.*, 81 (1974), 214–41.

SMITH, Steven B. "Relations of Inclusion," *Lg.*, 48 (1972), 276–84.

STOCKWELL, Robert P., Paul SCHACHTER, and Barbara Hall PARTEE. *The Major Syntactic Structures of English*. New York: Holt, Rinehart, and Winston, Inc., 1973.

THOMAS, Owen. *Metaphor and Related Subjects.* New York: Random House, Inc., 1969.

TYLER, Stephen A. *Cognitive Anthropology.* New York: Holt, Rinehart, and Winston, Inc., 1969.

VENDLER, Zeno. *Linguistics in Philosophy.* Ithaca: Cornell University Press, 1967.

VERKUYL, H. J. "Temporal Prepositions as Quantifiers," in *Generative Grammar in Europe*, ed. Ferenc KIEFER and Nicholas RUWET. Dordrecht: D. Reidel Publishing Company, 1972.

————. *On the Compositional Nature of the Aspects.* Dordrecht: D. Reidel Publishing Company, 1972.

WALMSLEY, John B. "The English Comitative Case and the Concept of Deep Structure," *FL.*, 7 (1971), 493–507.

WAUGH, Linda R. "The Semantics and Paradigmatics of Word Order," *Lg.*, 52 (1976), 82–107.

WEINREICH, Uriel. "Explorations in Semantic Theory," in *Current Trends in Linguistics*, Vol. III, ed. T. A. SEBEOK. The Hague: Mouton, 1966.

————. "Problems in the Analysis of Idioms," in *Substance and Structure of Language*, ed. Jaan PUHVEL. Berkeley and Los Angeles: University of California Press, 1969.

WIERCZBICKA, Anna. *Semantic Primitives.* Frankfurt: Athenäum Verlag, 1972.

————. "Why 'Kill' Does Not Mean 'Cause to Die': The Semantics of Action Sentences," *FL.*, 13 (1975), 491–528.

WILSON, Deirdre. "Presuppositions on Factives," *Linguistic Inquiry*, 3 (1972), 405–10.

————. *Presuppositions and Non-Truth-Conditional Semantics.* New York: Academic Press, Inc., 1975.

ZWICKY, Arnold M., and Jerrold SADOCK. "Ambiguity Tests and How to Fail Them," *Ohio State Working Papers in Linguistics*, no. 16 (1973).

Index

NOTE: A page reference in parentheses means the concept is discussed though the term is not used. For particular semantic roles—"deep cases"—see Role, semantic.

Abbott, B., 96
Absolute-process verb, 35
Accent, 105, 122
Accomplishment verb, 123, 125
Achievement verb, 35f., 65f., 122f., 125
Acquisition:
   case grammar, 72, 81
   comparatives, 62
   compound nouns, 53
   deictic terms, 102ff.
   evaluative adjectives, 59
   form and function, 20ff., 59
   indirect speech acts, 114
   kin terms, 19, 22
   mass/count, 31
   relative adjectives, 61f.
   temporal connectives, 66
   under-specified senses, 19, 103
Action, 34f., 123
Activity verb, 123
Adams, K. and N. F. Conklin, 42
Adams, V., 54, 61, 82
Adjectives:
   adverbial, 60
   dimensional, 63
   evaluative, 58ff.
   modalizing, 60f.
   relative, (58), 61f., 126f.
   temporal (= adverbial), 33
Adverbial:
   duration, (35), 63
   extent, 35, 63, 77
   manner, 18, 63
   means, 77
   purpose, 18, 77

reason, 77
Affix, 48, 123
Amalgamation rules, 66
Ambiguity/ambiguous, 1, 23, 29, 83, 85, 104, 123
Andersen, E., 20
Anderson, J. M., 60, 71, 76, 78f., 81, 101
Anderson, S. R., 106
Anglin, J. M., 11
Animacy/animate, 32, 72, 76
Anomaly/anomalous, 2, 22, 29f., 39, 42, 123
Associated components, 2, 14ff. (see also Component)
Austin, J. L., 108

Babcock, S. S., 81
Ballard, L., R. Conrad, and R. Longacre, 95
Bartsch, R. and T. Vennemann, 23, 67, 132
Beardsley, M. C., 42
Bennett, D., 73, 82
Bierwisch, M., 23, 62, 86, 91
Black, M., 42
Böer, S. E., and W. G. Lycan, 127
Bolinger, D., 26, 57, 67, 93, 122, 126, 128
Bowerman, M., 72, 81
Broad/narrow definition, 18, 22
Brown, R., 26, 81
Buckingham, H., 81

Campbell, R. N., and R. Wales, 63

147